CONTENTS

WORKSIGHT No.15 2020

Photo：中村力也

The Edge
［ジ・エッジ］

各フロアは建物中央に広がるアトリウムに対して開かれており、ここで働くワーカーの姿が互いに見える。「建物が生きている雰囲気」の感じられるスペースだ。

The Edge
アムステルダム [オランダ]
竣工：2014年
面積：約40,000㎡

スマートビルに「エクスペリエンス」を
取り入れたパイオニア

　スマートビルの新時代を切り開いた存在と知られるジ・エッジ。旧来の「スマート＝サステナビリティ」という図式に、ワーカーに豊かな「エクスペリエンス」をもたらすテクノロジーを導入した。ワークスペースの確保も、同僚の居場所の検索も、ロッカーやドアの解錠も、アプリ1つで。ジ・エッジは、ビル内で展開されるワークスタイルが1つのモバイルアプリで完結できる「APPセントリックワーク（アプリ中心主義の働き方）」の走りとなった。

　ジ・エッジはテナントビルだが、フロアの6割にデロイトが入居する。そのためビルの基本設計はデロイト仕様。前述のモバイルアプリも、デルフト工科大学発スタートアップだったMapiq（マピック）とデロイトとの共同開発だ。その恩恵をすべてのテナントが享受している。アプリ以外にも数社のスタートアップが提供するシステムでビル全体がマッシュアップされている点も新しい。「屋根がかかったコンピューター」の愛称通りの常にソフトウェアがアップデートされていくビルなのだ。

　ジ・エッジをスマートビルたらしめているのは、サステナビリティ、ウェルビーイング、スマートテクノロジー、ソーシャル・インタラクションの4点だ。

　まずサステナビリティについて、環境性能は、ヨーロッパの環境指標BREEAMで98.4％という世界最高水準の数値を示す。太陽熱の負荷が少ない北側にアトリウムを開き、ファサードの開口部を大きく確保。内部空間の配置を工夫したことで、約70％のデスクに日光が降り注ぐ。再生可能エネルギーも導入した。帯水層を使った地下130ｍの蓄熱冷暖房システムは、夏場に蓄積した温かい水を冬場に利用するもの。季節が変われば、そのプロセスを逆に。これにより膨大な量のエネルギーを節約できる。

　ウェルビーイングについても抜かりはない。ふんだんに降り注ぐ自然光は，ワーカーの幸福感、生産性、創造性の向上をもたらしてくれるもの。高級感あるレストランでは地域で生産された新鮮な食材が調理され、照明や室温は前述のアプリを通じてワーカー一人ひとりが調整できる。

　空間利用も効率的だ。実は、ビルの設計段階ではデロイトのワーカー3,100人に対してデスク数3,100席、床面積は5万㎡を想定していた。しかしその後リーマン・ショックに見舞われ、広さとコストのバランスを再考。4万㎡に1,000席、3,100人を収容する空間に見直された。その結果、ワーカー1人あたりの面積は減ったものの、業務内容に合わせてデスク、ソファ、スタンディング・デスク、ブースなどの作業空間を選べるABW（アクティビティ・ベースド・ワーキング）を導入し、働き方の自由度を高めた。贅沢なフィットネス・ルームなど、アメニティの充実も目を見張る。

　そして、冒頭で説明したアプリと、それが可能とするAPPセントリックワークは、スマートテクノロジーの産物ということになる。「スマートビルについて語るとき、多くの人がエネルギーの話をしますが、それはほんの一部にすぎません」とエリック・ウベル氏は言う。オフィス建築当時にデロイト側の責任者として企画にあたり、現在は、かつてOVGとして知られていたデベロッパーであるエッジのCTOに就いている。清掃やメンテナンスにかかるコストまで削減しつつ、利用者の満足度や生産性、ユーザーエクスペリエンスを向上させることがスマートテクノロジーの真の狙いだ。

　それを可能にするのは、天井に取り付けられた4種類、2万8,000個ものセンサーだ。この建物内ではあらゆるものがネットでつながっている。ワーカーのロケーション情報はもちろんコーヒーマシン1つとってもIoT化されており、階下のケータリング会社が管理している。清掃されているか、ミルクは十分か、コーヒー

1／中2階にあるラウンジ。開けた空間にもかかわらず音がうるさく響かないのは、吸音性の高い床材を採用しているから。あえてきれいに加工しないことで、音の跳ね返りを防いでいる。2／最上階近く、デロイトが専有しているイベントスペース。ここに置かれたコーヒーマシンもやはりIoT化されており、メンテナンスのタイミングが最適化されている。3／ジ・エッジ外観。ソーラーパネルが置かれた屋根は、太陽に向かって22度の角度で傾斜している。4／巨大なアトリウムは建物のエネルギー効率上昇に一役買っている。送風システムを稼働させなくとも、アトリウムを通じて温熱が建物全域に行き渡る構造。

自社開発のアプリが、あらゆる行動を司る

デロイトとデルフト工科大学発スタートアップ Mapiq が共同開発したアプリ。「新しいテクノロジーを開発するたびに新しいアプリをつくっていると、ワーカーがいくつもアプリをダウンロードしなければならない」。そこで1つのアプリに全機能を集約。座席の予約、卓上の照明や室温の調整も、すべてこのアプリで行う。トレーニングマシンによる運動の履歴なども残る。

©Ronald Tileman

©Horizon Photoworks

©Ronald Tileman

©Horizon Photoworks

©Raimond Wouda

©Horizon Photoworks

©Horizon Photoworks

©Horizon Photoworks

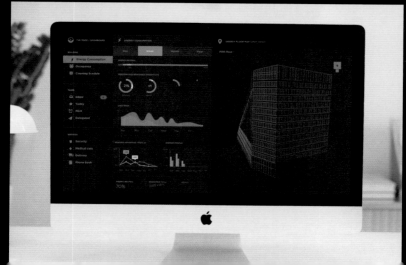

さまざまな情報を一元管理

天井に取り付けられた、2万8,000個のセンサーから建物全域のデータを集約。ファシリティの利用頻度、消費電力や室温、期待される生産性の数値などを、ダッシュボード上に表示している。

豆は補充されているか。答えがイエスなら、メンテナンスの手間も省けるというわけだ。同じように、誰もいないフロアは電気をシャットダウン。使われていないトイレならば、掃除をしない。

「コーヒーマシンやコピー機が壊れていたり、トイレが汚かったりしたら、人はハッピーな気持ちでいられません」

「私たちは、センサーを使って人を追いかけたりしているわけではありません。そう思う人もたくさんいますが、そういうことではないのです。建物がどのように使用されているか、どのようにエネルギーや清掃の効率を最適化し、利用者の満足度や生産性を向上させられるか。そこが大切です」

最後に「人をつなげる」ソーシャル・インタラクション。これは、スマートテクノロジー、サステナビリティ、ウェルビーイングの3点が高いレベルで維持されたとき、もたらされるものだという。例えば、空間をロスしているようにも思えなくもない巨大なアトリウム。だがここは、エネルギー効率の観点から見れば、温熱を建物全域に送る巨大な煙突の役割を果たしている。

「それに、たくさんの人々が働く姿を見渡せることで、建物自体が生きているような雰囲気があります。普通は、地上60Fにいる同僚がどんなふうに働いているかなんて、わかりませんからね。その同僚と直接話す機会がなかったとしても、姿が見えることで、同じ組織の一員だと思える。そのような感覚を、働く人たちは楽しんでいます」

デロイト自身は、このスマートビルからどのような恩恵を受けたのだろう。グローバルカンパニーはいま地球規模でタレントの争奪戦を繰り広げている。彼らはいまや、「単なる大企業」で働こうとは思わない。特にミレニアル以降の若い世代が求めるのは、楽しく過ごせ、生産性や満足度を向上させ、環境意識の高い職場なのだ。つまりそこでリアルに感じ取れる体験価値の高さこそがものを言う。

ジ・エッジは、若者たちの期待に応えるに十分だった。デロイトの人材募集には以前に比べ2.5倍の応募が来る。ワーカーの欠勤数は45%減少し、生産性は向上。一般的なビルに比べて、保守管理コストは40%減、電力消費量は70%減。竣工から5年を経て、スマートビルの効果は立証済み、と言っていいだろう。 **WS**

ジ・エッジがもたらした定量的効果

SMART TECHNOLOGY スマートテクノロジー	SUSTAINABILITY 環境	WELLBEING ウェルビーイング

BUILDING MANAGEMENT COST

 40% ↘

ビルのマネジメントにかかるコストが以前のビルと比べて60%に

ELECTRICITY COST

 70% ↘

以前のビルと比べるとわずか30%のコストで電気代を賄えるように

ABSENTEEISM

 45% ↘

病欠などを含む欠勤率が以前のビルと比べて45%減少

CAPITAL COST RETURN

 8.3 YEARS

資本コストは8.3年で回収

HEATING AND COOLING COST

 ±0

冷暖房にかかる費用がゼロに

EMPLOYEE SATISFACTION

 UP ↗

従業員の満足度が向上

SPACE OPTIMIZATION

 1,000 DESKS FOR 3,100

スペースの最適化により、約3,100人のワーカーに対してデスク数を1,000まで抑えることに成功

CARBON NEUTRALITY

 ±0

CO_2排出量を抑え、自然エネルギーを活用することでカーボン・ニュートラル（排出されるCO_2と吸収されるCO_2が同量）を達成

TALENT ACQUISITION / RISE OF DELOITTE APPLICATIONS

2.5x

The Edgeの稼働後、デロイトへ入社を求める応募者の数が2.5倍に増加

The Future of

Smart Workplaces

Edge Olympic Amsterdam / 22 Bishopsgate

Microsoft Netherlands / CIRCL

B. Amsterdam / Superblocks

スマートワークプレイスの未来

テクノロジーの発達によってオフィス、ビル、都市デザインのハイエンド化が進んでいる。スマートワークプレイスが向かおうとしている未来を、数々の事例を通じて探っていきたい。

個人に寄り添う
柔らかなスマートビル

Edge Olympic Amsterdam
［エッジ・オリンピック・アムステルダム］

A flexible smart building that
caters to the individual

ビル中央のアトリウム。コワーキング、スタジオ、サブテナントの専用フロア、デベロッパーであるエッジなどが入居する。中央の内部階段はユーザー同士がつながり、予期しない相互作用が生まれる1つのエコシステムだ。給水ポイントが設置されているのもサステナビリティ意識の高いオランダらしい。

同じアムステルダム、同じ開発・運営元。「エッジ・オリンピック・アムステルダム」と「ジ・エッジ」（2ページ）は、いわば双子のような関係にある。しかし、ジ・エッジがスマートビルのパイオニアならば、エッジ・オリンピックはスマートビルの最前線だと言えるだろう。

各種のテクノロジーには共通する部分も多い。照明や空調、会議室の予約などの機能を1つのプラットフォーム上に統合。コーヒーマシンの1つに至るまでIoT化し、建物内のデータを収集。ダッシュボードには建物のエネルギー消費や二酸化炭素排出量、音量、光量などが表示される。「今日は94.4%です」と、エッジCTOのエリック・ウベル氏は読み上げた。その日、ワーカーがどれだけ生産的になれるかを示す数字だ。当然、断言で

きるものではないが、建物自体がパラメーターを提示すれば、ワーカーも生産性を意識せずにいられないはずだ。これら最新のシステムを整えながら、エッジ・オリンピックは新築ではなく、古いビルを改修してつくられたテナントビル。潤沢な資金を持つ大企業でなくともスマートビルを手に入れられると示した事例でもある。

このビルを運営するのは、以前OVGとして知られていたエッジ。エッジ・オリンピックは当初からかなりの注目を集めていた。人がより生産的に、創造的に、幸福に働くために建物はどのようにあるべきか。その最新の答えが示されるものと、人々は期待したのである。

結果はこうだ。エッジ・オリンピックは人間が空間をコントロールするのではなく「空間自身が

GF（地上階）の共用ワークラウンジ。インスピレーション、リラクゼーション、コラボレーションと、求める機能に合わせてスペースを選ぶことができる。

人間に寄り添う」段階に達している。ウベル氏曰く、スマートビルには4つの段階があるという。

第1段階はデータの透明化だ。建物内のあらゆるデータを収集してダッシュボード上に表示したこと、1つのアプリを起点に室温や照明などの環境をコントロールできるようにしたことが、これにあたる。

第2段階は、データ同士のつながりを把握すること。例えば、重要なクライアントとの面会時間がわかれば、クライアントを優先的にエレベーターに案内することができるかもしれない。あるいは、

会議室の運用状況と各種のデータの相関を見ることで、人気の会議室とそうでない会議室の違いを発見できるかもしれない。「この会議室はいつも暑い、ここはとてもうるさい、角の会議室はいつも寒い。どうしてこれを変えようとしないのか不思議です。ビルのためにお金を払っているのに不便を受け入れてしまっている。私たちはそれを変えたい」(ウベル氏)。データの透明性がなかった時代は、暑い証拠、うるさい証拠を特定できず、改善を諦めなければならなかったところである。

第3段階は使用状況の把握だ。何人がどのよ

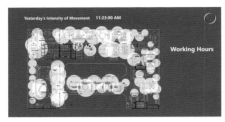

一定の時間内に、オフィス内でどれだけのワーカーがどれだけの場所を使ったかを示すデータ。よく使われる場所、使われない場所がひと目でわかる。

3Fのコワーキングスペース。天井裏には空調のための水冷式銅製パイプが通る。夏場は地下深くから汲み上げた冷水を流し、建物の熱を吸収している。

こちらもコワーキング。アトリウムに面した打ち合わせスペース。建物内はバイオフィリックで緑が多く、テクノロジーの存在をうまく隠している。ホワイトノイズなど音のコントロールもされている。

コワーキング内の会議室。音声アシスタントを通じてコーヒーなどをオーダーしたり会議環境をセットアップすることができる。

ウェルビーイングの一環として、健康的な食事を提供するレストラン。ライブ感あふれるオープンキッチンで食欲をそそる。

Edge Olympic Amsterdam
アムステルダム［オランダ］
竣工：2018年
面積：12,367㎡

1

2

4

3

5

1／デベロッパーのエッジが入居しているフロア（2〜5も同フロア）。既存ビルに木造架構の2フロアを増設した。ホームライクな家具の印象と相まって健康的な雰囲気を感じ取ることができる。

2／レセプション。テクノロジーが発達することで仰々しいレセプションが不要となることを示す好例だ。

3／会議室。ここでも音声アシスタントが常駐しており、話しかければオンライン会議をセットアップしてくれたりする。

4／シックで清潔なトイレ。男女兼用、全個室としたのは、男女別トイレに戸惑うことがあるLGBTQなどセクシュアル・マイノリティへの配慮から。

5／フロアでは案内ロボットが走り回っていた。

データ活用のための4つの段階

第4段階
Machine Learning
マシンラーニング

↑

第3段階
Usage Analysis
使用状況の把握

↑

第2段階
Data Correlation
データの相関性

↑

第1段階
Data Transparency
データの透明化

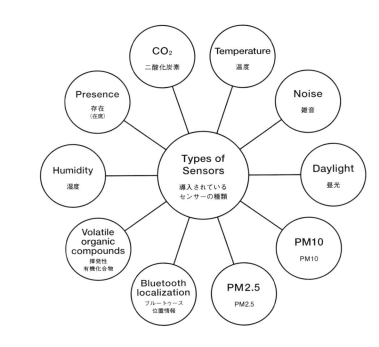

CO₂
二酸化炭素

Temperature
温度

Presence
存在
(在席)

Noise
雑音

**Types of
Sensors**
導入されている
センサーの種類

Humidity
湿度

Daylight
昼光

Volatile
organic
compounds
揮発性
有機化合物

PM10
PM10

Bluetooth
localization
ブルートゥース
位置情報

PM2.5
PM2.5

デスク下に見える赤いランプがセンサー。これがデス
クの利用状況を把握している。レイアウト変更、清掃
プランの効率化など空間利用価値の最適化につながる。

17

1

2

3

4

うにその部屋を使っているのか、わかっている状態を指す。一見単純そうに思えるが、実は難しい。センサーの判断は「空いている席」でも、人間が見れば「荷物が置いてあるから、使用中」と判断されることもままあるからだ。実際には体温を感知するセンサーやカメラを通じて判断するという。その際、個人を特定しないような配慮がなされていることは必須だ。

そして第4段階がマシンラーニングだ。第3段階までに蓄積させたデータを統合し、アルゴリズムを発見する。エッジ・オリンピックはこの第4段階にある。ジ・エッジと同様、システムを支えているのは天井や家具に設置されたセンサーだ。だがその数はセンサー10種類が合計6万5,000個とジ・エッジの2倍以上。これがありとあらゆるデータを拾い上げる。続いて、データをもとに仮想空間上のデジタルツインでシミュレーションを行い、その結果をリアル世界にフィードバック。こうして、ワーカーの行動、エネルギー消費やメンテナンス、清掃などの最適解をビルが自律的に導くのだ。人に寄り添う空間のあり方をビル自身が学び、ビル自身が実行してくれるという、スマートビルの最前線。現在世界各地で「エッジ」ブランドのプロジェクトが進行中だ。スマートビルの代名詞となる日もそう遠くない。**WS**

エッジ・オリンピック外観。1928年アムステルダム・オリンピックのスタジアム近くに位置する。都心の喧騒から離れた落ち着いたエリアだ。既存ビルに木造の2フロアが増設されているのがわかる。

エッジ
CTO
エリック・ウベル

Erik Ubels
CTO
EDGE

1／エントランス。ビルに入った瞬間に小さなレセプションとカフェが来訪者に迎え入れる印象を与える。スマートテクノロジーによってレセプションは門番からコンシェルジュのような役割に。

2／GF（地上階）、階段状のシアターエリアがビル全体の共用部としてある。外部にイベントとして貸し出されることもあり、取材時は大学のプログラムが行われていた。

3／ビルに入居するEpicenter（エピセンター）のレセプション。Epicenterは欧州中心にスタートアップ育成に定評のあるコワーキングブランドだ。

4／ビル内のロッカーはアプリで検索、解錠を行うことができる。

5／GFのロビー。ビル全体の共用部としてミーティングスペース、タッチダウン・デスクなどが置かれている。バイオフィリックな環境がリラックスした雰囲気を感じさせる。

5

高さ278 m、62階建て。超高層ビ
ルが立ち並ぶロンドン中心部の金
融街シティ・オブ・ロンドンに位置
する。アイコニックではなく、多面
体で風景に溶け込むデザインは、
地域貢献への意志の表れだ。オー
プンは2020年夏の予定。

CASE 2

ロンドンの街に溶け込む
バーティカル・ビレッジ

22 Bishopsgate
［トゥエンティトゥ・ビショップスゲート］

A vertical village that blends in
with the City of London

Levels 58 - 61

RESTAURANT, BAR AND VIEWING GALLERY
レストラン、バー、ビューイング・ギャラリー

一般に開放される58 Fのビューイング・ギャラリー。ロンドンの街並みを一望できる。24時間営業のレストランも。

Level 41

THE RETREAT
ザ・リトリート

身体や精神の健康をケアするためのフロア。ヨガのレッスンなどが行われるスタジオ、病院や歯科医院なども入る。

Level 7

THE EXCHANGE
ジ・エクスチェンジ

ワーカーが行き交うコワーキングスペース。スタートアップ向けに低価格帯でデスクを提供する。プロ仕様のレコーディングルーム、カンファレンスに対応できるスペースも完備する。

Level G

Lobby
ロビー

レセプションのほか、半年ほどで展示が変化するギャラリーがある。地下には1,700台分の駐輪場、サイクリング・コミュニティのためのバイク・パークやコミュニティ施設も備える。

Level 57

THE CLUB
ザ・クラブ

高級感のあるビジネス・ラウンジ。ダイニングとしてはもちろん、会議にも使われる。

Level 25

THE GYM
ザ・ジム

ジム内にはクライミング・ウォールや高地トレーニング専門の部屋を完備。ダンスなどのグループ・クラスができる部屋など、さまざまな活動を異なる料金帯で提供。

Level 2

THE MARKET
ザ・マーケット

フロア全体にフードホールが広がる。テラスでの食事も楽しめる。フードコートは常時変化があり、すぐ食べられるサンドイッチから3コースの食事まで用意。定期的に入れ替わるポップアップ・レストランも。

ロンドンを代表する金融街であるシティ。その中心に新たなランドマーク、「22 Bishopsgate（トゥエンティトゥ・ビショップスゲート）」が建設中だ。

設計はジ・エッジと同じくPLPアーキテクチュア。同社が手がけるビルがたびたびそうであったように、今回も、マルチテナントビルの未来の形を示すものになる。その理由は「アメニティシェアを備えたバーティカル・ビレッジ」という新しい試みだ。

「テナントはアメニティを自分のスペースに置きたくないのです」と、ビル構想に関わったアンワークのCEOであり未来学者のフィリップ・ロス氏は言う。そこで約12万㎡の延床面積に約1万㎡の共有アメニティスペースを置いた。コワーキングスペースにクラブ。ジムはクライミングウォールや高地トレーニング専用の部屋を備える。「リトリート」は心身をリラックスさせるスペース。レストランは朝昼夜それぞれ3つのコースを用意し、毎日通う利用者を飽きさせない。「世界中のどのマルチテナント・オフィスビルにも、このスケールはないと思います。仕事はもちろん、食べたり飲んだり運動したり、リラックスしたり人と交流したり。人々がビルを家のように考えてくれればうれしいですね」（ロス氏）

アメニティ・シェアの仕組みが特に響いている

22 Bishopsgate
ロンドン［イギリス］
竣工予定：2020年
面積：約120,000㎡

ワークスペースのイメージ。内部階段もリクエストに応じて開けることができる。多面的なファサード、かつ鉄分の少ない高透過ガラスを使うことで自然光を多く取り入れ、ウェルビーイングにも配慮されている。

フレキシブルなフロア設計

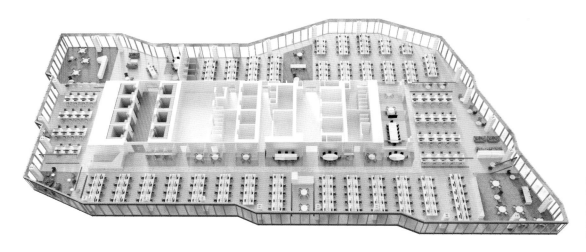

同一フロアに最大4つのテナント
が入ることを想定し、さまざまな使
い方ができるよう各フロアはフレ
キシブルな設計にしてある。キー
テナントを入れるよりもSMEの多
様性を優先した形だ。

スマートビルの進化形態

Lv. 5	**The True Smart Building** 真のスマートビル
	↑
Lv. 4	**Sensorization** 感覚への対応
	↑
Lv. 3	**Contextualization** 人の動きに応じた提案
	↑
Lv. 2	**Individualization** 個別状況への対応
	↑
Lv. 1	**Efficiency** 効率性の高さ

ユーザーがいる。第一にミレニアル以降の若い世代。22ビショップスゲートは、彼らが共有するシェアの価値観をテナントビルに持ち込んだ。第二にSME（中小企業）。これまで、充実したアメニティと言えば一部の大企業のみのものであり、それが採用面での競争力に影を落としていた。だがアメニティ・シェアの形なら小さい企業でも優秀な人材を惹き付けられる。ビルサイドもSMEを受け入れることでビルや都市に多様性や新しい価値観を持ち込むことができる。

デベロッパーには「バーティカル・ビレッジ」のビジョンがあった。アメニティが入るフロアを区切りに4層のビルを積み上げ、1万2,000人がビル内を縦横無尽に働く共同体をつくり上げる構想だ。

そこには、「パブリックに開かれたビル」という狙いもある。

「アメニティの数を増やし、パブリックな領域を建物内に取り込むことは、クライアントの希望であるだけでなく、都市からの注文でもありました」。そう語るのはPLPのファウンディング・パートナー、カレン・クック氏。成長する街ロンドン、その中心部にあるシティ・オブ・ロンドンは過去10年間で通勤者数を10万人以上増やし、今後も同じペースでの成長が見込まれている。しかしそれは働く場だけが供給されたドライなものであり、ワークとライフを統合する新世代のワーカーが期待するものではなかった。「人は、ほかの人と接したいものです。テクノロジーによって在宅で働くことが

可能となる一方、孤立することでメンタルヘルスの問題が悪化している。人は他人と接することで得る刺激が必要で、企業も人々にともに仕事をしてほしいと考えています」（クック氏）。これを受けて、職場に関して新しいアイデアを考えると同時に、増える労働者、自動車、自転車を考慮し、都市環境の中でどのように責任ある存在でいられるか探ってもいた。「すると、人々が職場に対し、よりよいソーシャルな場を求めていることがわかったのです」（クック氏）

端的に言えば、このビルはロンドンの街に溶け込もうとしている。超高層ビルが個性を競い合うロンドンにあって、多面的で柔らかく控えめな外観もそうした意図からだ。展望台も一般市民に開放される。「ロンドン中、イギリス中、そして世界中の人たちにロンドンの高層ビルを体験してもらえます」（クック氏）

都市環境において責任ある存在としてのビル。ときには利便性より社会的責任を重視する姿勢も見せる。都市の自動車を減らしストリートに人の流れを取り戻す一括配送の取り組みが一例だ。すべての配達物はいったん郊外の倉庫に運ばれたのち、倉庫とビルを行き来する小さな低排出車両で配達される。デベロッパーであるリプトン・ロジャース・ディベロップメンツのポール・ハーグレーヴス氏によれば「この規模の大きさのビルだと、1日1,000回の配達があってもおかしくないですが、一括配送により30回に減らせるかもしれません」ということだ。

テクノロジーに関しても、グローバルにスマートビルを調査しロードマップを描いている。レベル1はエネルギーやお金に関する効率性。レベル2はワーカー一人ひとりに対する個別化、最適化。ワークスペースや室温が一例だ。レベル3は「文脈化」。データをもとに、ワークスタイルやワークフローをビルの側が人々に提案する。レベル4になると今度は「静かな時間を設けたほうがいいのでは」「日光を浴びたほうがいいのでは」といった、24時間周期のリズムに応じた感覚面まで踏み込んでビルが提案してくれる。そしてレベル5はビッグデータの活用による、ビルそのものの最適化。真のスマートビルと呼べるのは、レベル5に達したビルと結論付けている。「テクノロジーが追いついていないので、まだ誰も5にはたどり着いていないと思います。私たちは確実に3には達しているというところでしょうか」（ハーグレーヴス氏）。それでも、将来5まで上がれるようにセットアップができていることを彼は期待している。

真のスマートビルの姿を見据えながら、テクノロジーの追求は今後も続く。しかし彼らの視線は常にヒューマンサイドに注がれている。**WS**

7Fのコワーキングスペース「Exchange」では、セミナー、学習コース、イベントの豊富なプログラムも開催される。新しい考えやアイデアを学び、共有するための専用スペースが充実している。

1／GF（地上階）は、オープンで魅力的な新しい歩行者環境を実現。4つのメインエントランスがあり、キュレーションされた絵画や彫刻が来訪者を出迎える。

2／クロスビー・スクエアへの入口。足元にはグリーンをふんだんに植え、アスファルトをナチュラルな石貼りに替えることで、過ごしやすい空間に。

3／にぎやかなビショップスゲート通りに面したメインエントランス。無料展望台に24時間営業のレストランと、一般市民を受け入れるビルらしくオープンなデザイン。アートが施され、ビル風を軽減する大きなキャノピーが特徴だ。

4／フードホール。オープンキッチン、フードキオスク、レストランとテラスバーがあり、食事、待ち合わせ、リラックスなど、さまざまな選択肢を用意。親しい人たちのための「Speakeasy」も。

5／ワーカーは顔認証で入館可能。ビジターには電子パスが送られる。レセプションはアートやライブラリーといった滞在時間を豊かにする機能などコンシェルジュ的な役割に変化。

6／専用アプリを通じて仕事環境をカスタマイズ。例えばブラインドの開閉もアプリから行える。アメニティフロアの食事を各フロアまで直接オーダーすることも可能。

1

4

2

5

3

6

アンワーク
CEO
フィリップ・ロス

Philip Ross
CEO
UnWork

リプトン・ロジャース・ディベロップメンツ
建設ディレクター
ポール・ハーグレーヴス

Paul Hargreaves
Construction Director
Lipton Rogers Developments

PLPアーキテクチュア
ファウンディング・パートナー
カレン・クック

Karen Cook
Founding Partner
PLP Architecture

「テクノロジー × ヒューマン」で
スマートビルはどう変わるのか

PLP Architecture

**How technology x people will change
the future of smart buildings**

PLPアーキテクチュア
代表取締役
リー・ポリサノ

Lee Polisano
Founding Partner & President
PLP Architecture

英国登録建築家、米国登録建築家。PLP
アーキテクチュアの創業者であり、これ
まで40以上の高層・超高層タワープロジ
ェクトを手がける。その多くが持続可能
で環境性能に優れた建築であり、国際的
に高い評価を受けている。

ス　マートビルの設計事務所と言えば、まず「PLPアーキテクチュア」の名が挙がる。ジ・エッジ、22ビショップスゲートを手がけたのも同社だ。PLPのこれまでと、彼らが見据える未来のオフィスについて尋ねた。

　PLPの設立は10年前のこと。代表のリー・ポリサノ氏ともう一人の共同パートナーはかつて世界的な設計事務所KPF（コーン・ペダーセン・フォックス）で仕事をしてきたが、フィロソフィーの違いから離脱を決めた。以来、都市とのコラボレートやパブリックスペースの使い方、人が集まるスペースのつくり方を考えてきたのが彼らである。

「私たちが信じているのは、『優れたイノベーションや関係、アイデアというものは、2人の人間がコミュニケーションをしなければ起こらない』ということです」。そんなコミュニケーションに貢献できるビルをつくれたら、それは世界のコミュニティに貢献していることになる。

　「世界の医療研究を20年進めた」と言われるクリック・インスティチュートを設計したのもPLP。クリック・インスティチュートには2019年にノーベル生理学・医学賞を受賞したピーター・ラトクリフ氏をはじめとするノーベル賞クラスの研究者を含む1,250人が集まり、新しいがん研究を行う施設だ。その信念はここでも裏付けられている。

　リサーチをベースに設計を進めるのも、よく知

PLPアーキテクチュアはロンドンに拠点を置く建築設計事務所。次世代のスマートビルを提案する。執務フロア中央のメインストリートには光天井が走る。

られるPLPの特色だ。都市や文化、ビルの利用者、テクノロジーを自ら研究し、その都市、そのビルにふさわしいコンセプトを開発する。「建築家の役割を少し考え直す、というところではないでしょうか」。通常、建築家は多くの専門家の知識をまとめる人間として存在する。だが、ポリサノ氏が描く建築家像は違う。「未来に向けて社会を前進させる役割を、建築家が担えると思っています。また、建築家のようなヒューマニスティックなアプローチをしている人がその役割を果たさなければ、テクノロジー中心のアプローチをしている人が社会を独裁していくという懸念もあります」

この言葉から察しがつくように、ポリサノ氏の関心は「テクノロジー」ではなく、「人」に向かっている。スマートビルを設計するにあたっても、中心には人を置く。振り返ってみれば、ジ・エッジからテクノロジーを取り除いたとしても美しいビルであり、ワーカー同士が出会い、予期せぬ相互作用が生まれる場所であることには変わりがない。しかし、そのビルとテクノロジー、スペシャルなコンセプトを組み合わせることで、テクノロジーの可能性がより広がる。「私たち建築家には、そんな想像ができるんです。テクノロジーの力も、スペースの力も理解している。その力を合わせたと

きにどうなるかも、理解しているからです」。例えばそれが、環境性能の向上による「持続可能なビル」であり、ウェルビーイングを取り入れることで人々がより幸福に働けるビルなのである。

もっとも、すべてを独自にリサーチしようとはしていない。やはり刺激的なコミュニケーションを求めて、各分野のトップとのコラボレーションを重視する。リサーチ・プロジェクトは「PLP Labs」として、一部が公開されている。例えば、ケンブリッジ大学の自然素材イノベーションセンターと

PLPのオフィス内、執務フロアの様子。オープンオフィスに並べられたシンプルなロングデスクで所員が作業に励む。

PLP本社オフィス。スマートビルを数多く手がける彼らの住処は予想を裏切るクラシカルなアールデコ調のビル。ロンドンの所員は約150名でワンフロアを占有している。

デスクの間に設けられたコミュニケーションスペース。さまざまな職能を持ったエキスパートたちが協働し、都市における新しい建築をつくり出す。

1

2

3

4

1／リサーチ・プロジェクトの1つ「NuMo」。自動運転技術を応用したオンデマンドで排出のない自律的な大量輸送をサポートする都市モビリティ・システムを提案している。

2／こちらもリサーチ・プロジェクトである「CarTube」。既存道路とは別に自動運転車専用の地下トンネルを張り巡らせることで効率的かつ都市に人間的空間を取り戻す。

3／超高層ビルでの垂直輸送の可能性を追求した「SkyPod」。建築外部にリニアモーター技術を応用し、さまざまな方向への移動、内部空間のフレキシビリティを実現。

4／「Oakwood Timber Tower 2」。ケンブリッジ大学の自然素材イノベーションセンターとのコラボレーションで木造高層建築の可能性を追求する試み。

のコラボレーションにより「Oakwood Timber Tower 2」と題した高さ130ｍの木造建築の提案が話題を呼んだ。またPLPは、カーボンゼロを目指したロッテルダムの高さ140ｍの木材ハイブリッド・ビルの国際コンペティションにも勝っている。

　PLPは今後、どのようなポジションを築いていくのだろう。スマートビルが普及するに従って、強力なコンペティターとなる設計事務所も現れるはずだ。「コンペティションにどう勝つかとか、そういうことをあまり考えていないですね。考えるのはどうやって差別化できるか、どうしたら楽しんで仕事ができるか。どうやってこの組織を第2のステージへ成長させるか、世界が向かっている変化にどう対応するか、そんなことです」

　だが、ポリサノ氏はこうも言った。

　「会社として私たちが物理的、経済的にだけでなく知力的にも成長するための施策が、日本に事務所を開くことでした。日本の社会は新しいアイデアや研究に基づいて次世代の商品やアイデアに役立つ情報を提供しようとしています。だからこそ私たちもそこにいることで日本に貢献しながら学びを得ることができると感じたのです」**WS**

ロンドンはキングス・クロスにある世界的ながん研究の施設「クリック・インスティチュート」。研究者同士のコミュニケーション・トリガーのためにヴィジビリティ（視認性）を重要なファクターとして設計された。

PLPアーキテクチュアが見据える
スマートビルの未来

左
PLPアーキテクチュア
ファウンディング・パートナー
ロン・バッカー

Ron Bakker
Founding Partner
PLP Architecture

PLPアーキテクチュアの共同創業者。建築におけるテクノロジーの役割や、都市に与える影響に造詣が深い。世界中の大学や、不動産、都市開発、TEDxを含む建築のデジタルテクノロジーに関するフォーラムで講演している。

右
PLPアーキテクチュア
パートナー
相浦みどり

Midori Ainoura
Partner
PLP Architecture

イギリス、アメリカ、ヨーロッパ、中東、アジアの各地で、オフィスや住宅、学校、マスタープランニング・プロジェクトなどの設計に20年以上にわたって従事。アムステルダムのスマートビル「The Edge」の建設ではデザインを主導した。

「スマート」といえばデジタルテクノロジーのみを指していたのは昔のこと。今やあらゆる形でワークプレイスを改善し、人間がよりよく働くためのファシリティすべてを意味するようになった。PLPファウンディング・パートナーのロン・バッカー氏はそう考えている。

スマートビル実現の手段も移り変わる。「5年前、ワークプレイスで重要だったのは快適さや持続可能性、きれいな空気、それからある程度の技術でしたが、今は神経科学や社会科学、また人と人のコラボレーションの仕方へと変わってきています」(バッカー氏)。また、働き方の変更も見逃せない。デジタルが手作業を代替したことで、人はより創造的で、コラボレーションを必要とする「人間らしい仕事」に注力するようになった。「オフィススペースは、従来の『仕事のため』のスペースではなくなり、ますます『人間のためのスペース』になっています」

それでも、テクノロジーが役割を終えたわけではない。センサーが二酸化炭素濃度や室温、照明、自然光を測定することも重要だ。しかしより重要なのは、そうして得られたデータをどう使うか。「本当にスマートなビルでは、単に環境だけを測定するのではなく、環境と仕事の質、そして人々の幸福との関係を見て、理解しようとします」。それが成功すれば、よりよい仕事、よりよい幸福を得る方法が見えてくる。

「空気中の二酸化炭素が多すぎると、頭が痛くなり、仕事のペースがスローダウンしてしまう。それなら二酸化炭素を測定し、調整するのがいいでしょう。また自然光はいいものと思いがちですが、自然光でストレスを感じる人もいて、そういう人は薄暗い部屋の方が快適です。このように、テクノロジーのおかげで環境と人間をよりよく理解できるようになる。これが未来だと思います」

とはいえ、誰にとっても健康なビルが実現できるかといえば……。「いい質問ですが、はっきり言って無理です」とバッカー氏。さまざまな人の

さまざまなニーズに応じて、さまざまな空間をつくる。必然的に、働く場所の選択肢はより増える方向へと進むだろう。にぎやかな場所にいたい人も、静かな場所で働きたい人もいる。その両方のニーズに応えなければならない。

「そうでないとおかしいでしょう。会社にとって最も高価なものは人です。自動車を製造していれば違いますが、オフィス環境の中では、家賃よりも、家具よりも、テクノロジーよりも、食べ物よりも、コーヒーよりも、一番お金をかけているのは人間です。人間が最も高価で、最も重要です」

インペリアル・カレッジ・ロンドンが人間の幸福度に影響を与える要素を研究したところ、「人を最も不幸にしているのは仕事」という結論が出た。だからこそワークプレイスの改善は難しい。逆に幸福度や生産性の鍵になるのは「エンゲージメント」だったという。エンゲージメントとは、自分も組織の一員であると感じるかどうか、自分が評価されているかどうか、ということ。要するに「自分

「スマート」の価値提供とシステムの発展イメージ

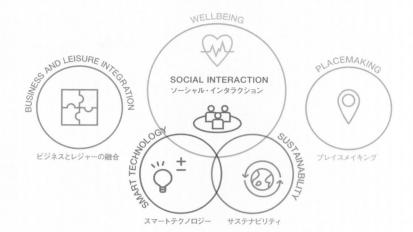

BUSINESS AND LEISURE INTEGRATION
ビジネスとレジャーの融合

WELLBEING

SOCIAL INTERACTION
ソーシャル・インタラクション

PLACEMAKING
プレイスメイキング

SMART TECHNOLOGY
スマートテクノロジー

SUSTAINABILITY
サステナビリティ

COMMUNITY CENTRIC コミュニティを中心とした価値提供

SOCIAL INTERACTION ソーシャル・インタラクション	SOCIAL INTELLIGENCE ソーシャル・インテリジェンス	FIND INTERESTING PEOPLE 興味のある人を見つける
PLACEMAKING プレイスメイキング		ORGANIZE GROUP ACTIVITIES グループのアクティビティの整理

PEOPLE CENTRIC 人間を中心とした価値提供
Wellness ／ ウェルネスの向上を目指す

BUSINESS AND LEISURE INTEGRATION ビジネスとレジャーの融合	WELLNESS BOOST ウェルネスの向上	ENCOURAGE PERSONAL WELLBEING 個人のウェルビーイングの促進

PEOPLE CENTRIC 人間を中心とした価値提供
Room Environmental control & wayfinding ／ 室内の環境制御など

WELLBEING ウェルビーイング	AMBIENT INTELLIGENCE アンビエント・インテリジェンス（環境知性）	ADOPT TO ME 自らのものとして取り入れる
		FIND WHAT I NEED 何が必要かを見つける
BMS ビルディング・マネジメント・システム	EGRESS, SIGNAGE, SECURITY, PRESENCE 人の出入り、導線、セキュリティ、存在（出席）の管理	ONSITE SERVICES 出張による保守サービス
		SPACE UTILIZATION スペースの活用
		EASE OF ACCESS アクセスのしやすい導線

FACILITY CENTRIC ビルの保守管理を中心とした価値提供

SUSTAINABILITY サステナビリティ	POWER, AIR, WATER, DATA 電力、空調、給水、各種データの管理	ENERGY MANAGEMENT エネルギーの保守管理
		EQUIPMENT MANAGEMENT 設備の保守管理

FUTURE ↑ CURRENT

の仕事にとても興味があり、仕事に対してワクワク感があった方が明らかにいい仕事をします」。そしてエンゲージメントには、ワークスペースや建築のクオリティ、ロケーションなどが影響する。

PLPパートナーの相浦みどり氏も、これから「スマートテクノロジー」「サステナビリティ」は当たり前のものになるため、むしろスマートビルには「ソーシャル・インタラクション」「プレイスメイキング」「ビジネスとレジャーの融合」がより重要になると語る。生活の延長線上に仕事を位置付け、ワークプレイスを都市にちりばめ、人間中心の場をつくることがエンゲージメントを高める方向に作用するだろう。

「ある神経科学者によれば、人が窓を開けたり、家具を動かしたりして自分の環境を変える機会を与えれば、その人の認知過程が25％改善するとのこと。人々がともにワークプレイスをつくる『co-creation』が将来のキーワードになると思います」（バッカー氏）**WS**

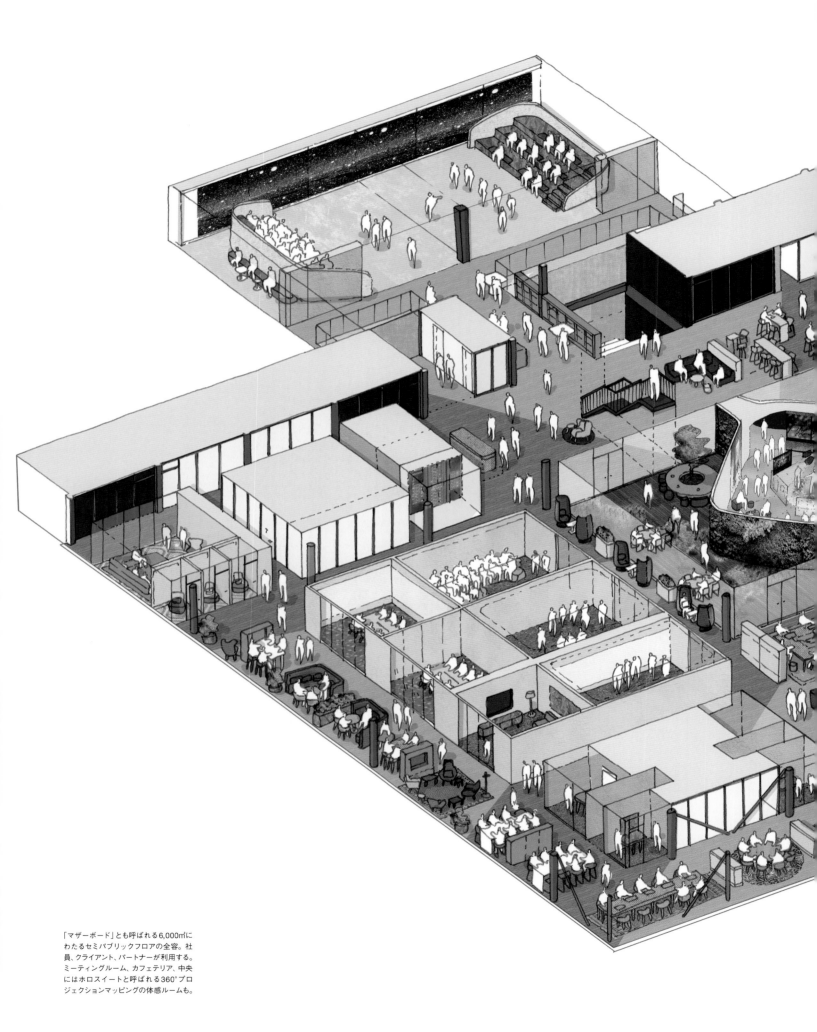

「マザーボード」とも呼ばれる6,000㎡に
わたるセミパブリックフロアの全容。社
員、クライアント、パートナーが利用する。
ミーティングルーム、カフェテリア、中央
にはホロスイートと呼ばれる360°プロ
ジェクションマッピングの体感ルームも。

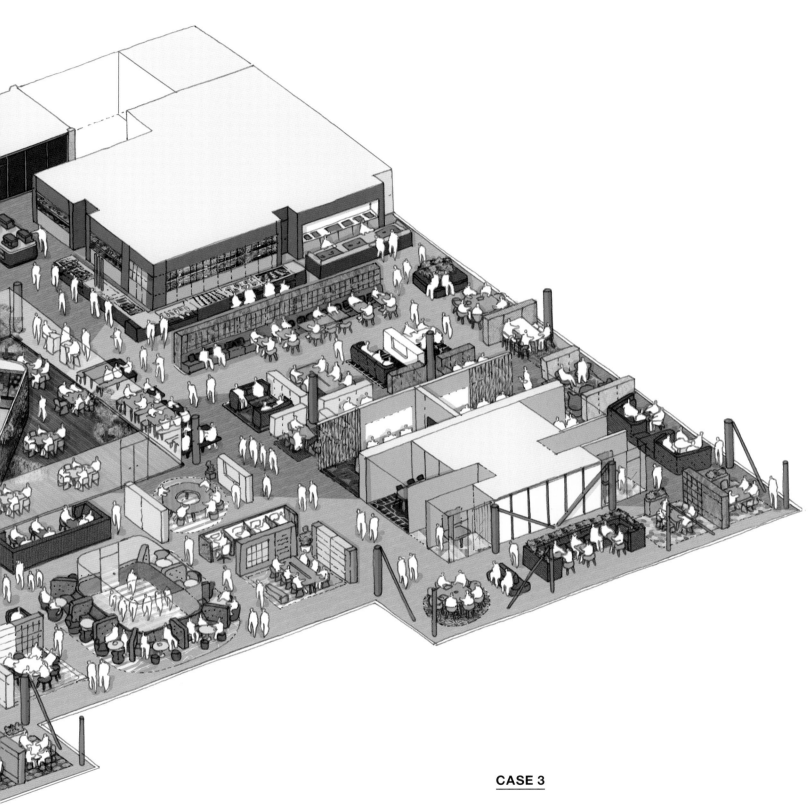

CASE 3

小さなコミュニティづくりを促す
「マイクロポリス」

Microsoft Netherlands

［マイクロソフト・ネダーランド］

The "Micro Polis" —
encouraging small-scale community building

1／マイクロソフトの社員だけが入れるプライベートスペース。社員もセミパブリックスペースを利用できるが、集中したいときはここで。日本の畳が敷かれた小上がりも。

2／セミパブリックスペースの、一段階セキュリティが高いエリア。ゲストと社員が利用できる。フロアは感性を刺激するアートにあふれている。

3／オフィス外観。このテナントビルに入居したのは12年前。ビルの契約更新のタイミングだった2017年の夏に「もっとクライアント向けのスペースが必要だ」と大がかりな改修を行った。スキポール空港近くのエキシビションセンターやオフィスビルが立ち並ぶエリアに位置する。

4／セミパブリックエリアにある、開放感あふれるカフェスタンド。各種アメニティを、マイクロソフトの社員、ゲスト、スペーシーズの利用者がシェアすることも、コラボレーションを促す契機になる。

Microsoft Netherlands

アムステルダム［オランダ］
創業：1975年
従業員数：13万1,000人（2018年）
売上高：1,103.6億ドル（2018年）
※各種データはマイクロソフト全体のもの

3

マイクロソフト・ネダーランド
ビジネス＆デジタルトランス
フォーメーション・リード
ディレクター
レネ・ファン・デル・ヴュルジュ

René van der Vlugt
Director
Business and Digital
Transformation Lead
Microsoft

ディー・ドック
クリエイティブ・ディレクター
兼 パートナー
フランシスコ・メッソーリ

Francesco Messori
Creative Director and
Partner
D/DOCK

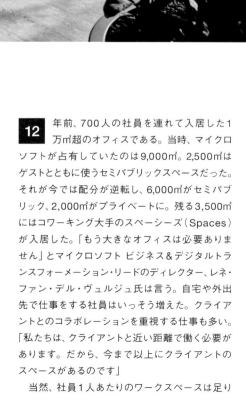

4

12 年前、700人の社員を連れて入居した1万㎡超のオフィスである。当時、マイクロソフトが占有していたのは9,000㎡。2,500㎡はゲストとともに使うセミパブリックスペースだった。それが今では配分が逆転し、6,000㎡がセミパブリック、2,000㎡がプライベートに。残る3,500㎡にはコワーキング大手のスペーシーズ（Spaces）が入居した。「もう大きなオフィスは必要ありません」とマイクロソフト ビジネス＆デジタルトランスフォーメーション・リードのディレクター、レネ・ファン・デル・ヴュルジュ氏は言う。自宅や外出先で仕事をする社員はいっそう増えた。クライアントとのコラボレーションを重視する仕事も多い。「私たちは、クライアントと近い距離で働く必要があります。だから、今まで以上にクライアントのスペースがあるのです」

当然、社員1人あたりのワークスペースは足り

セミパブリックのワークスペースの一部。ここはリラックスできるソファ席。1日を快適に過ごせる場所なら、仕事のパフォーマンスも最大化する。

クライアントやパートナーに開かれたオフィスへ

2007年

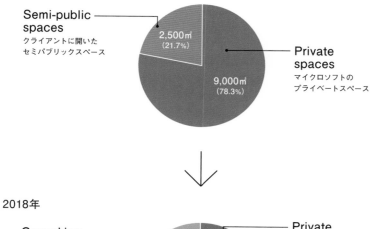

Semi-public spaces
クライアントに開いた
セミパブリックスペース

2,500㎡
（21.7%）

Private spaces
マイクロソフトの
プライベートスペース

9,000㎡
（78.3%）

2018年

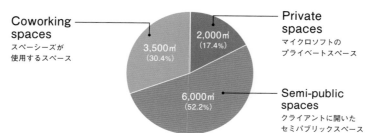

Coworking spaces
スペーシーズが
使用するスペース

3,500㎡
（30.4%）

Private spaces
マイクロソフトの
プライベートスペース

2,000㎡
（17.4%）

6,000㎡
（52.2%）

Semi-public spaces
クライアントに開いた
セミパブリックスペース

1／セミパブリックのワークスペースの一部。個人やチームがこもって集中できるようカーテンやパーティションで区切られたスペースも。「気分に合う場所をいつも見つけられる」とヴュルジュ氏は言う。

2／エントランス。セキュリティは必要以上に厳格ではなく、ゲストを歓迎している。左に見えるキッチンでコーヒーを飲みながら迎えを待つ。配布されるIDでロッカーの解錠、カフェテリアでの飲食などもスムーズに行える。

3／ゲストと社員が共用するレストラン。健康的な食事が提供される。スペーシーズともシェアすることでファシリティの効率化を図る。

4／セミパブリックスペースの一部。社員とクライアントがじっくりコラボレーションするためのエリア。フロアごとにデザインテイストが変えられ、個室、キッチンなども長時間滞在に耐えられるしつらえに。

なくなるが、そこにスペーシーズを組み合わせた。スペーシーズは、ABWによって季節や時間帯によって増減する社員が利用できるバッファスペースなのだ。もう1つ重要な役割がある。マイクロソフトが注力している人工知能系スタートアップの誘致に活用しているのだ。

オフィスのコンセプトは「マイクロポリス」。「オフィスはコミュニティです。他者と出会い、ものを共有し、予期しないことに出くわす場所です」とインテリア設計を担当したディー・ドックのクリエイティブ・ディレクター、フランシスコ・メッソーリ氏。建物内にさまざまな空間を設けることで、違った価値観を持つ者がそれぞれの「ポリス」に集い、好みのワークスペースで有機的につながる過程で小さなコミュニティを生み出す。デザインが同じ部屋がないのもそのためだ。

改めて、この革新の理由をヴュルジュ氏に尋ねた。1つはワークライフバランスのコントロールだ。自宅でもできる仕事を会社に持ち込む必要はなく、休息中にメッセージをチェックする必要もない。「仕事をもっとがんばるのではなく、スマートにしなければいけない。それが私たちのとった、単純な方針です」。もう1つの理由はクライアントとのコラボレーションにある。各クライアントとのコラボレーションの形に応じて、各チームの働き方も変わる。より自由度が高く広い空間が求められるのは、自然の流れだった。

マイクロソフトはテクノロジーの会社だ。当然ながらデジタルテクノロジーによるスマート化も進めている。1,000カ所以上のセンサーが室温や照明、湿度、二酸化炭素濃度、部屋の使用状況を把握し、社員の居場所を追跡する。「現在はIoTソリューションに注目しているフェーズです」（ヴュルジュ氏）。センサーをどうしたらもっと賢くできるのか。ビル全体の暖房をどうコントロールするのか。寒い日に早く室温を上げることはできるのか。データの用途はいくらでもある。会議室の予約などオフィス内のオペレーションを改善するにも役立つ。実際、マイクロソフトでは42%の定例会議が事前に予約された部屋で起きていなかった。「どのようなプロセスで、どうしたら人々の行動を変え効率的にできるか、見ています」

ホスピタリティもここでは重要なテーマだ。「私の意見だとホスピタリティは、仕事環境の未来です」（メッソーリ氏）。ホテルのようなスイートルームを設けたのが一例だ。ベッドとバスルームこそないが、クライアントやチームが1〜2日こもって仕事をしたり、休息したりするのに十分なものが揃っている。テーブルとチェアしかない会議室では1時間も働けば疲れてしまう。しかしスイートルームなら、仕事はもっと快適になるだろう。彼らはオフィスを「ブレジャー」と呼ぶ。ビジネスとレジャーをかけ合わせた言葉だ。ここでは両者がハイブリッドしている。「私たちはハイブリッドをあらゆる場所でやったのです」（メッソーリ氏）

オフィスはもはや働くためのただの箱ではなくなり、多種多様な働き方を支える「パーソナル・アシスタント」として生まれ変わったのだ。**WS**

1

2

3

4

1／コワーキングスペース、スペーシーズの一角（2〜6も同施設）。外部からやってくるゲストとマイクロソフト社員が交じり合う。

2／少人数で利用するミーティングブース。手前はパーソナル・デスク。あらゆるニーズに応えるワークスペースが用意されている。

3／オープンエリアにあるカフェスタンド。気さくなスタッフとの会話が弾む。

4／明るい窓際のソファシート。スキポール空港にも近く、グローバル・カンパニーが集積する計画都市の眺望が望める。

5／スタートアップが入居する個室も。スペーシーズは拠点ごとに個性があるが、ここにはマイクロソフトがコラボレーションを望む人工知能関連のスタートアップを中心に誘致している。

6／エントランス。パステルカラーを基調とした柔らかい雰囲気が来訪者を迎える。

データ分析がワークプレイス・デザインに
もたらす変化とは

Zaha Hadid Architects

**Data analytics meets
workplace design**

ザハ・ハディッド・アーキテクツ
コンサルタント
ウリ・ブラム

**Uli Blum
Consultant
Zaha Hadid Architects**

オランダの建築会社OMA Asiaに勤務し、
ゲーリー・テクノロジーズの香港オフィ
スのプロジェクト・ディレクターとして
2011年にザハ・ハディド・アーキテクツ
（ZHA）に入社。現在は以前 Foster +
Partnersのパートナーだったアルジュン・
カイカー氏とZH Analytics + Insights
（ZHAI）の共同経営者を務める。

1

2

3

1／ザハ・ハディッド・アーキテクツ本社オフィスのエントランス。レセプションとカフェテリアが一体となっており、所員のリフレッシュやパートナーとのミーティングなどに使われている。

2／本社オフィスのボードルーム。クライアントとの重要なミーティングにも使われる。

3／本社オフィスの執務スペース。2016年に亡くなったファウンダーのザハ・ハディッド氏が使っていたデスクが当時のまま置かれている。

4／オフィス外観。ロンドンのデザインファームが集積するクラーケンウェルにある元小学校を改修したもので、事務所開設から一貫して入居している。ロンドンだけで約400名の所員が働く。

「データはオフィス設計をどう変えるか」。ザハ・ハディッド・アーキテクツの「Analytics + Insights」はこの問いを探求するプロジェクトだ。ウリ・ブラム氏と彼の同僚、アルジュン・カイカー氏とで2015年にスタートさせた。彼らは建築家だが、コーディングと計算の才能を持ち合わせていた。「データのないデザインは単なる装飾。さらに、データなしに設計することは、目隠しして運転しているようなものです」とブラム氏は言う。「ワーカーの健康とパフォーマンスへの影響を分析せずにデザインを決定することは、方向性に欠け、危険ですらあります」

彼らのアプローチは、Netflixのような企業が時間の経過とともにユーザーの好みを学習して改善する方法と似て、ユーザーデータをマイニングするオンラインサービスから学習してユーザーのニーズと好みを予測すること。これは、機械学習を使用して、職場の満足度と好みに関するデータを継続的に分析することにより、オフィスに応用できる。

「そのようなオフィスがあったら、それがより幸せで、健康的で、より成功に近いワーカーとビジネスを生み出すと強く信じています」

昨今のオフィスはセンサーを導入し、ビルの使用状況に関してデータを集めようとしている。し

さまざまなパラメーターを用いて綿密なシミュレーションを行う

1

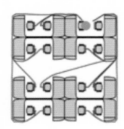

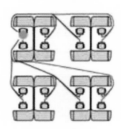

3

Average Humidity

100%
75%
50%
25%
0%

Mon, Jan 22

Average Temperature (℃)

32
24
16
8
0

Mon, Jan 22

Average CO2 (ppm)

1200
900
600
300
0

Mon, Jan 22

Desk Occupancy

100% Peak
75%
50% Average
25%
0%

Fri, Jan 19　Sat, Jan 20　Sun, Jan 21　Mon, Jan 22　Tue, Jan 23　Wed, Jan 24　Thu, Jan 25

2

43% of desks <8mts away

73% of desks <8mts away

複雑なデータ分析を実行するために、元となる空間利用に関するデータを収集する。

1 デスク形状によって視線や距離がどのように変化するかを示した図。
2 データを応用すると、レイアウトによってワーカー同士の距離感がどれだけ変化するか理論値を算出できる。
3 センサーを使うことで温度、大気質、机の占有率などの変数を監視して、机が実際にどのように使われているかをリアルタイムで測定できる。

4

Arts University of Bournemouth | Lower Exhibition Space
24 Hour Movement Sensor Reading

00:00:00

ZH Analytics and Insights

6

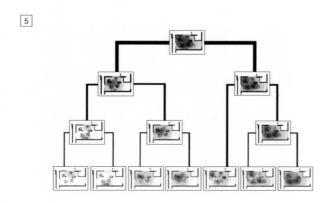

5

7

Distance to Daylight Source (DS)

Total: 55.5　Average: 0.67

Visible Area (VA)

Total: 29.28　Average: 0.46

Integrating DS + VA

Total: 42.39　Average: 0.66

4 ギャラリーで実施したセンサーによる行動データ取得。空間の利用頻度が高い部分が赤く「ヒートマップ」として表示される。
5 ヒートマップを分析することで、利用シーンを科学的にグルーピングすることができる。
6 外部形状とコアの位置を機械的に分析し、一瞬で数万通りの解析を行うことができる。
7 建築のコアをどの位置に持ってくるのが最適か、日光までの距離と可視領域をもとに分析した図。

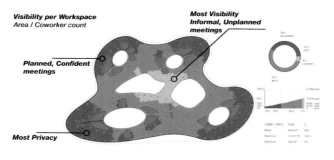

Visibility per Workspace
Area / Coworker count

Planned, Confident meetings

Most Visibility Informal, Unplanned meetings

Most Privacy

Galaxy SOHO, Beijing
Zaha Hadid Architects

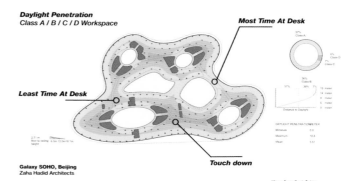

Daylight Penetration
Class A / B / C / D Workspace

Least Time At Desk

Most Time At Desk

Touch down

Galaxy SOHO, Beijing
Zaha Hadid Architects

Views From Each Table
120 Degree Cone of View

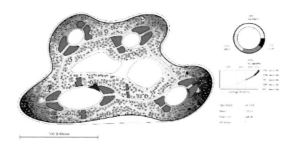

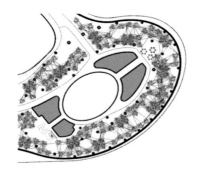

設計を手がけた北京にあるマルチテナントビル「ギャラクシー SOHO」で実際に使われたデータ分析。ワーカーから見た視認性、移動距離、彩光、眺望などをパラメーターとして変化させることでどのような影響が出るか、何十万というシミュレーションを重ねた。一見、恣意的に見える形状やコアの位置もこうした綿密な分析によって、合理的な解として導き出されている。

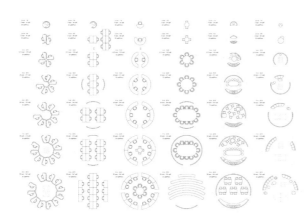

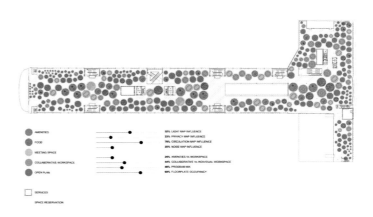

同じくZHAが設計した広州にあるオフィスビル「インフィニタス・プラザ」では、ZHAIが開発したアルゴリズムを用いてオフィスレイアウトの自動化を行っている。レイアウトは、利用人数とシーン（集中と会話）に基づいてシフト。センサーでスペースの使用頻度を監視した後、パラメーターを調整し、レイアウトを自動的に更新できる。このプロセスを繰り返すことで、空間自体がセルフラーニングするようになる。

かしそのデータから、ビルだけでなく働く人のパフォーマンスの最適化に役立つような識見を見出すことには至っていない。

「ビルのライフサイクル・コストは1%が建設費用で、9%がメンテナンスとエネルギー、そしてワーカーへの給与が90%です。つまり、働く人の満足度や生産性を10%向上させることは、ビルを10棟建てるのと同じ効果があるということです」

データは、人々のコラボレーションや育成にも好影響をもたらす。「たとえば、MITのトーマス・J・アレン教授は、デスクの位置が離れるとコミュニケーション率が下がるという研究結果を発表しています。8m離れるとコミュニケーションは減少し始め、24m以上離れるとほとんど会話は生まれません」。彼らはオフィスのデスク間の距離を測るアルゴリズムの開発を通して、レイアウトの微妙な変化がオフィス内の交流に影響することがわかった。また、フロアの角にあたるエリアには

あまり人が集まらないということも発見した。「残念ながらたいてい、企業はその位置にボスの席を置きます」。皮肉にも、最もコミュニケーションが起きにくい位置に、だ。

オフィス空間を最適化するにあたってもう1つ大事なのがデスク同士の関係性だ。当然、自分と向き合っている人とコミュニケーションをとるのは簡単で、また多くの場合、自分からは見えない人に見られている状態を不快に感じるものだ。この視覚的ネットワークは人の心理的快適性に大きな影響を与える可能性があるが、これまでほとんど分析されてこなかった。

「私は中国と香港に住んでいたことがありますが、レストランの丸いテーブルには驚きました。テーブルにいる全員がほかの全員を平等に見られるため、コミュニケーションにプラスの影響を与えていました」。彼らは、さっそくこの事実を反映したアルゴリズムをつくり、さまざまなレイアウトの

分析を行っているという。これによりデスクの配置によってワーカー同士の可視性をはかり、それぞれのデスクに視覚的快適性を測るスコアがつけられ、これをもとにオフィスのレイアウトを再構成することができる。

もっとも、データが豊富なら必ず唯一無二の答えが導けるとは限らない。「以前は何か基準をつくってオフィス全体に展開すれば全員が幸せになるはずだという考えがありました」。しかし今日では、むしろ重要なのは多様性だ。照明も室温も人の好みは一様ではない。「ですから、企業は多様な環境を提供しないといけません」

データはオフィス設計をどう変えるか。ブラム氏の提案は「設計者が直感ではなくデータに基づいてよりよい意思決定を行うこと」だ。彼は直感に任せるより、データを用いる方が優れた判断を導き出すと考える。建物は、単純化された仮定や時代遅れのスタンダードに基づいて設計される

1／本社オフィスから徒歩10分ほど離れた、ブラム氏とZHAIが入居するオフィス。建築家のほか、数学者やデータサイエンティストなども含まれる。国際コンペティションのプロポーザルを扱うチームも同じフロアに入居する。

2／GF（地上階）ギャラリー。ザハ・ハディッド氏がデザインした家具やオブジェなどを中心に展示。地下はエキシビションスペースで、いずれも一般に開放されている。

3／Analytics + Insights チームが入居するオフィスの外観。路面に面した開放的なビルをギャラリー、オフィスとして3フロア使っている。

のではなく、膨大な量の入力とパラメーターに基づいて設計できるようになった。「テクノロジーを使うことで、設計についてより詳しく知ることができ、よりよい決定を下すことができます」

　データに基づいたオフィス設計という新たな分野を独学で開拓してきた彼ら。今、目指すゴールは「自動的に最適化されるオフィス」だ。そしてそれは、センサーに自動設計アルゴリズム、移動式の家具が揃えば可能だ。それぞれのユーザーのニーズに合わせて自ら変化し、セルフラーニングするワークスペースのネットワーク。すべてを備えたオフィスは、まるで生命のサイクルのように変化、進化を繰り返すだろう。「照明が1日のうちに色が変わったりするというのはすでにやっていることです。でも家具の色が変わってもよい。例えば春、桜が咲く頃は白っぽくして秋は土をイメージさせるような色合いとか。冬は鬱々しないよう明るい感じがいいですね」 **WS**

CASE 4

大手金融機関が見せる
サーキュラー・エコノミーへのリーダーシップ

CIRCL

［サークル］

A major financial institution takes
a lead in the circular economy

TOILETS

フロア全景。写真右側にはサステ
ナビリティに配慮されたグッズを
販売するショップ、奥が廃棄物ゼ
ロを目指すレストラン。左がワーク
ラウンジの一部。空間の大半はリ
サイクル資材を使用している。

3

4

5

6

CIRCL
アムステルダム［オランダ］
竣工：2017年
面積：3,500㎡
利用企業数：約2,000社（2018年）

1／外観。アムステルダムのビジ
ネス地区、ザイダスに位置する。
後ろにそびえるのがABNアムロ銀
行の本社ビル。ここを本拠地とす
る大手銀行だ。

2／ギャラリー。GF（地上階）には
ギャラリーのほか、ワークラウンジ、
ショップ、レストランが入っている。

3／地下。ミーティングやワークシ
ョップの部屋が並ぶ。ABNのワー
カーのほか、市民や外部団体が利
用することも。サステナブルな未
来の都市像を模索する大規模イベ
ント「We Make The City」のメイ
ン会場としても使われた。

4／地下のミーティングスペース。
取材時には、行員にサーキュラー・
エコノミーの価値観を伝えるサー
クル・アカデミーのワークショップ
が行われていた。

5／地下のカフェスタンド。イベン
ト中のブレイクに、クライアントと
のカジュアルなミーティングにと
多用途に使われる。

6／地下のイベントスペース。もと
もと銀行にあった金庫や私書箱な
どを持ち込み、木質の意匠を施し
インテリアとして生まれ変わらせた。

1

3

2

4

1／環境負荷を考慮し、冷蔵庫はできるだけ使わない。食材は特別なケースを使って油や酢に漬け込むなどして常温のまま保存されている。

2／1F（日本でいう2Fに該当）にあるバー。自分たちでつくった地ビール、地元のラムやジン、茶にこだわっている。施設で頻繁にイベントが開催されるため、そのレセプションでも活用される。

3／1Fのバーから、ガーデンへ。レストランの生ゴミは肥料として使用。すべてオランダの植物で、季節ごとに異なる表情を見せる。

4／CIRCLの裏手。通りに面した階段状のシアタースペースは市民の憩いの場として親しまれている。

5／レストラン。ゴミを最小限にする「Zero Waste」を実践しており、フードマイルの少ない地元から仕入れた食材を徹底的に使い切る。健康面でもケアしており、ヴィーガン・メニューも豊富。

リ ニアな経済成長を目指す資本主義の象徴ともいうべき銀行が、持続可能な社会の中で自らの存在意義を模索している。「利益のためではなく、社会にいい影響を与えるため」（CIRCL［サークル］のディレクターを務めるメリン・ファン・デン・バーグ氏）、ABNアムロ銀行は欧州における持続可能なサーキュラー・エコノミー（循環型経済）のリーダーになろうと動き出しているのだ。

きっかけは偶然だった。CIRCLのプロジェクトチームが動き始めたとき、ちょうど、ミーティングルームの不足に対処するためにABN本社オフィスを拡張する計画が既に進んでいたのだ。その結果が世界最高水準の持続可能レベルを達成する

ことを目的とするビル、CIRCLだ。ABNの行員だけでなく外部の関係者も利用できる10室のミーティングルームを備えているほか、ワークショップ、レストラン、ギャラリーなどが一般公開され、地元の市民が集う。

環境負荷を最小限にするため、大半の資材は別の建物で利用されたものをリサイクル。天井の防音・断熱材は1万6,000着の使用済みジーンズやペットボトルを細かく刻んだものだ。置かれている家具はヴィンテージを扱うパートナーから提供された。

さらに、すべての建築部材には固有IDとデータベースで情報が管理され、解体後の再利用まで視

野に入れている。CIRCLのインテリア面で助言を行ったカルトーニ・デザインのファウンダー、マリン・ミューラー氏も「無毒の接着剤を使用するので、いつでも分解し、再利用できます」と話す。

レストランも語るべきことが多い。食材はすべて地元の農家から提供されたものを使用。季節折々の食材を前に、シェフは毎日メニューづくりに知恵を絞ることになる。「私たち自身で蜂を飼っており、蜂蜜を自作しています。ここにはたくさんの花があるため、とても上質な蜂蜜がつくれるんですよ。レストランで発生した食材のゴミは庭の土に還して肥料に変えている。すべてが円（サークル）になってつながっているんです」（バーグ氏）

CIRCLの建築に関わるバリューチェーン

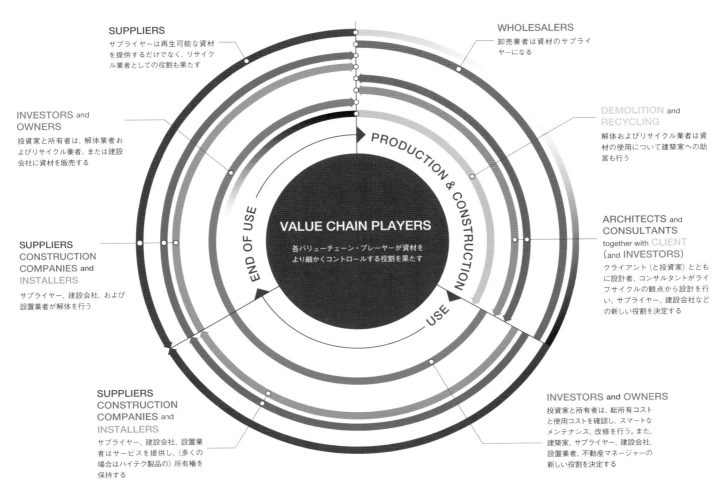

© Circle Economy, Architekten Cie and Circl

CIRCLの建築にあたって設計されたバリューチェーン。各プレーヤーが従来以上の役割を果たすことで、環境負荷の小さな循環経済を構築することができる。

CIRCL が投資したさまざまな環境技術

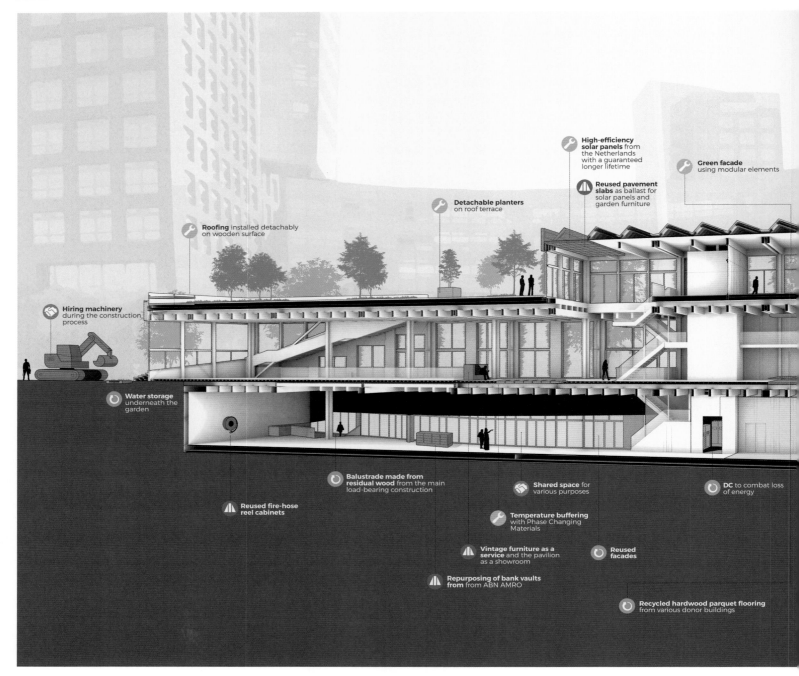

Roofing installed detachably on wooden surface

Detachable planters on roof terrace

High-efficiency solar panels from the Netherlands with a guaranteed longer lifetime

Reused pavement slabs as ballast for solar panels and garden furniture

Green facade using modular elements

Hiring machinery during the construction process

Water storage underneath the garden

Reused fire-hose reel cabinets

Balustrade made from residual wood from the main load-bearing construction

Shared space for various purposes

DC to combat loss of energy

Temperature buffering with Phase Changing Materials

Vintage furniture as a service and the pavilion as a showroom

Reused facades

Repurposing of bank vaults from from ABN AMRO

Recycled hardwood parquet flooring from various donor buildings

CIRCLの建物にはさまざまな環境技術が投下されており、この図はそれを示したもの。設計と運用にあたっては、可能な限りCIRCLの持つビジネスモデルが使用されたという。

サークル
ディレクター
メリン・ファン・デン・バーグ

Merijn van den Bergh
Director
CIRCL

カルトーニ・デザイン
ファウンダー
マリン・ミューラー

Marijn Muller
Founder
Cartoni Design

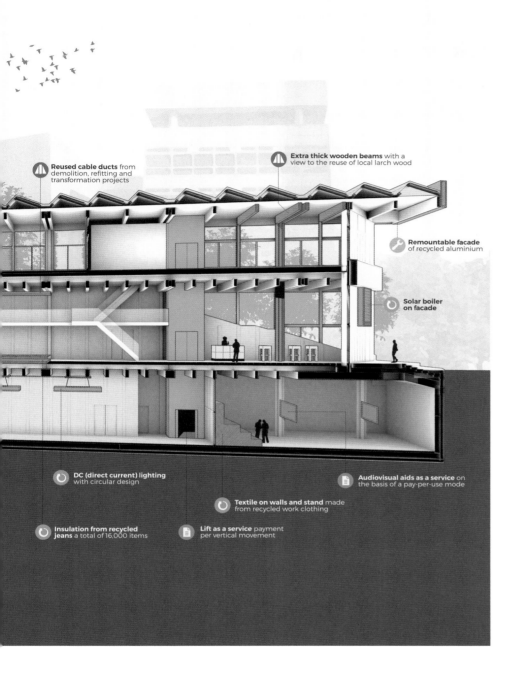

Reused cable ducts from demolition, refitting and transformation projects

Extra thick wooden beams with a view to the reuse of local larch wood

Remountable facade of recycled aluminium

Solar boiler on facade

DC (direct current) lighting with circular design

Audiovisual aids as a service on the basis of a pay-per-use mode

Textile on walls and stand made from recycled work clothing

Insulation from recycled jeans a total of 16,000 items

Lift as a service payment per vertical movement

CO₂排出量の大幅な削減に成功

RENEWABLE ENERGY
再生可能エネルギー

28.1t

CIRCLでは、再生可能エネルギーを生成・供給することにより、年間28.1トンのCO₂排出量削減に成功した。28.1トンのCO₂は、アムステルダム、パリ間を飛行機で200回移動した際に生じる量に相当。

WOODEN CONSTRUCTION
木造建築

594t

CIRCLの主な構造は鉄筋コンクリートではなく、木材である。木材を利用することで年間594トンのCO₂排出量が削減できる。アムステルダムからマドリードへ自動車で912回往復した際に生じる量に相当。

MATERIAL REUSE
資材の再利用

813t

新しい資材の製造や輸送を回避し、資材の再利用を徹底。これにより年間813トンのCO₂排出量削減に成功した。これは電車でアムステルダムからローマへ3,939回移動した際に生じる量に相当。

のみならず、ゴミを最小限にする「Zero Waste」ポリシーを掲げており、ゴミが出ないようにシェフは工夫を凝らして材料を使い切る。「野菜がメインですが、シェフに何が提供されるかによって肉や魚も使います。繁殖しすぎたために政府に処分された鹿の肉などを提供することもあります」(バーグ氏)。そして食材の保存には油や酢で漬け込むことで常温保管。ここでは冷蔵庫を必要としていないのだ。

CIRCLはABNアムロのワーカーからクライアント、地元住民ら、誰もが立ち寄れる場所だが、ワーカーにサーキュラー・エコノミーを教育する場でもある。「サークル・アカデミー」がそれだ。1年

で3,000人もの行員がプログラムを受けるほど活発に展開している。ゆくゆくは外部にもアカデミーを公開する予定だ。アカデミーの参加者は、将来何をすれば社会がよくなるかを考えている。どうすれば自分の家も持続可能になるか、どうすればビジネスも持続可能になるか。

ワーカーたちの反応はどうだろう。

「やらなくてはいけないということをみんなが知っています。当社にはアカデミーがあり、知識を持った先輩行員も多くいます。新しいスタッフがサーキュラー・エコノミーを理解するための環境はとても整っていると言えます」(バーグ氏)

彼自身、以前は持続可能性のことを全く知らな

かったという。たとえゆっくりでもワーカーを教育することの大切さを説いてくれた。「そうすれば自身の家で意識することもできます。クライアントと話すときも、できるだけ持続できるモデルを考えようと努力するでしょう。強要はしませんが提案はします。我々の知識を、クライアントのために役立てたいのです」(バーグ氏)

サーキュラー・エコノミーのリーダーになるとのスタンスはCIRCLを通じて世に提示され、好意的に受け入れられた。新たに生じた多様なステークホルダーとの「循環」は行員を変え、彼らのビジネスそのものを変えるだろう。それこそCIRCLの本当の価値だと彼らは信じている。 **WS**

コワーキングスペース兼カフェテリア。ここはオープンスペースだが、フリーランスや企業が入居する個室も建物内にはある。カフェテリアはコミュニティを育むハブとして重要な役割を担っている。

CASE 5

欧州最大級のビジネス・プラットフォームは
「スマートシティ・ゾーン」へ

B. Amsterdam

［ビー・アムステルダム］

One of Europe's largest coworking companies
builds a smart city

かつてはIBMがオフィスとして使っていたビル一棟をすべて改修した「B.1」。スキポール空港に近いこともあり、周囲にはオフィスと物流系の倉庫が点在する。

個人用のデスクが並ぶエリア。フリーランスが多く利用している。

コワーキングスペースの一角にあるミーティングスペース。ソファが数台並んだ、リラックスした雰囲気。

GF（地上階）にあるカフェテリア。奥には大規模なイベントスペースも設けられており、入居者以外のコミュニティづくりにも貢献している。

1／かつてこの建物をオフィスとして使っていたIBMが借りている「IBM Innovation Space」。彼らも新しいアイデアのためにスタートアップとのつながりを求めている。

2／IBMの執務スペース。ビニールハウスのような簡易的な設えで部屋が構成されている。

3／旅行代理店Hotelchampが大きく借りているエリア。フリーランス、スタートアップ以外に100人以上の規模の企業も入居する。

4／スタートアップ・ブートキャンプのオフィス。アクセラレーター・プログラムで有望なスタートアップを育てる活動をしている。

5／最上階、5Fにあるレストランのバーカウンター。GF（地上階）のカフェテリアはセルフサービスだが、ここではフルサービスが受けられる。

6／レストランに隣接するルーフトップパーク。1,600㎡の規模でハーブなどの野菜を育てている。

B. Amsterdam
アムステルダム［オランダ］
竣工：2015年
面積：約40,000㎡
入居企業数：約300社（2018年）

1

4

2

5

3

6

欧州最大級のコワーキングだ。近くに固まって建つ4万㎡、3棟の建物は入居者で完全に埋まり、300社以上のスタートアップ、大企業、フリーランスが集う巨大なプラットフォームと化している。それでも1万5,000㎡分のウェイティング・リストがあるというから、恐れ入る。コワーキングはテナントビルの一部を利用する形態が一般的だが、3棟丸ごと1つのブランドのもとで再編されるケースはおそらく世界でも類を見ない。

この敷地は、かつてIBMのオフィスだった。IBMが退去した後、10年以上は廃墟のまま。これをリノベーションし、誕生したのがB. Amsterdam（ビー・アムステルダム）だ。「当時は完全に空のビルで、コンクリートしかなかった。水も電気もな

いところから始めました」とB. Amsterdamコファウンダーのリカルド・ファン・ルネン氏は言う。資金もなく、廃校になった古い大学からチェアやシェルフなど多くの家具を譲り受けてインテリアを構築した。

ルネン氏は「私たちのプラットフォームは、人をつなげ、人を集め、成長するためにあります」と語り、センサーなど最新テクノロジーを導入したスマートビルには、どちらかといえば批判的だ。曰く、センサー自体がビルの中にいる人々の働き方を変えるわけではないし、人々を結び付けるわけでもない。部屋の温度を管理するより、つながるのに適した人々がいたほうがもっと幸せかもしれないと、ルネン氏は考える。

「スマートシティ・ハブ」内部。広大なスペースがエリア全体のエコシステムを構築することに活用される。

「B.1」に隣接する倉庫を改修した「スマートシティ・ハブ」。スマートシティにまつわるスタートアップを誘致し、敷地内にサーキュラー・エコノミーを構築する計画を進めようとしている。

3棟あるうちの1つ、「B.3」。かつて日産自動車が使っていたが、やはりビル一棟すべてを改修した。写真は地上階のカフェテリア。健康的な食事が提供されている。

ユーザーもまた、そう考えているのだ。ここにはコワーキングスペースがあり、大小のスタートアップが入居するプライベートオフィスがあり、その点ではウィーワークをはじめとするコワーキングと大差ないかもしれない。だが、充実したファシリティや「スマート」なテクノロジーも、B. Amsterdamの本質ではない。何より重要なのは、ここでは人々が有機的なつながり、コミュニティが育っているという事実である。入居しているのは、メンバーにふさわしく「ともに成長できる」と認められた者のみ。そして彼らによって構成されるコミュニティが、また新たなメンバーを惹き付けるのだ。オフィス内でのミートアップや各種のカンファレンス、ワークショップなども、彼らの交流を促している。

「ウィーワークは不動産の会社だと思っています」とルネン氏。B. Amsterdamはそうではない、と彼は強調しているのだ。「私は不動産に愛はないのですが、人々の成長は愛している。これは異なるマインドセットですね」

B. Amsterdamの一員になるべく大企業も押し寄せている。現在はハイネケンやPwC、FIFAなど、17社が入居しているという。かつて自分たちのオフィスとして使用していたIBMも入居しているというからおもしろい。彼らは皆、スタートアップとの協業を求めている。その周囲ではスタートアップらがエコシステムを形づくる。

「スタートアップもクライアントを必要としていますし、大きな会社の力が必要です。彼らは、ともにいることで繁栄することができるのです」

2014年にスタートしたB. Amsterdamは、ルネン氏も驚くほどのスピードで成長した。だが現在までのところ、B. Amsterdamのコミュニティは建物内に押し込められている。これをエリア全体へと拡張するプランがある。「スマートシティ・ゾーン構想」がそれだ。

ステップ1として、現在は1,800㎡の農場をつくっているところだ。ゆくゆくは、農場で育てられた食材を敷地内のレストランで提供するようにもなるだろう。廃棄物も再利用する。続いて、住宅を建て、少ない水、少ない電気で暮らしていく。倉庫を改修した「スマートシティ・ハブ」に、スマートシティ関連のスタートアップを誘致する。とにかく持続可能な街をつくるためのあらゆるソリューションを試みようとしている。

「私たちの最初の夢は、ビルの中に街をつくることでした」とルネン氏。だが、その夢は早々に実現してしまった。「今は、未来ある街をつくることが私たちの夢です。そのために一生懸命働いています」 WS

ビー・アムステルダム
コファウンダー
リカルド・ファン・ルネン

Ricardo van Loenen
Co-Founder
B. Amsterdam

1／「B.3」外観。壁からせり出した
ように見える部分が写真2のボー
ドルームだ。

2／「B.3」のボードルーム。ビル全
体の共用会議室で、入居企業がそ
の都度レンタルして使用する。

3／「B.3」の共用部には現代アー
トが多数飾られている。カジュア
ルな「B.1」と比べて洗練されたイ
メージを訴求している。

4／「B.3」に入居する企業のプラ
イベートオフィスが並んだフロア。
グリーンや木材のフローリングが
ナチュラルな印象をもたらしている。

1

2

3

4

ワークテック・アカデミー
ディレクター
ジェレミー・マイヤーソン

Jeremy Myerson
Director
Worktech Academy

FOCUS 3

「ビル」「シティ」に代わる
スマートの新しい単位「プリシンクト」

The Smart Precinct

**A new unit for building "smart"
that will transform the city of the future**

ワークプレイス研究の世界的権威。ワークテック・アカデミーのディレクター、ロイヤル・カレッジ・オブ・アート（RCA）ヘレン・ハムリン・センター・フォー・デザインの特任教授も務める。韓国、スイス、香港のデザイン機関の諮問委員会にも参加。

コンセプトは「インターミックス」

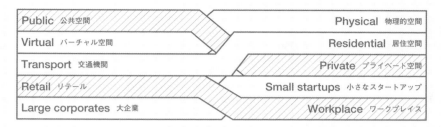

Public 公共空間	Physical 物理的空間
Virtual バーチャル空間	Residential 居住空間
Transport 交通機関	Private プライベート空間
Retail リテール	Small startups 小さなスタートアップ
Large corporates 大企業	Workplace ワークプレイス

インターミックスとは、バーチャルとリアル、大企業とスタートアップ、公と私といった、
対立するさまざまな要素を結合させる概念を指す。

社会の変化に伴い、デベロッパーの役割も変わる

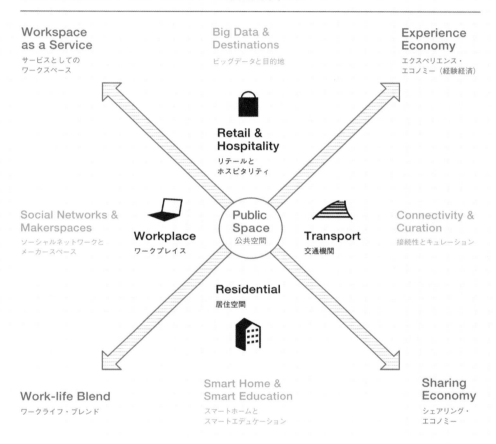

インターミックスが、働き方のトレンドや新技術にどう呼応するかを示した図。例えば、
スマートフォンのアプリやデジタルチェックインは職場でもサービス業でも活用が進む。

「ス マート・プリシンクト」は、ワークプレイス界の権威ジェレミー・マイヤーソン氏がオーガナイズする研究プロジェクトの1つだ。

ここで注目するべきは「スマート」の単位である。つまり街区（プリシンクト）のサイズだ。スマート・プリシンクトは2〜3ブロック、1つのデベロッパーが管轄しているエリアをテクノロジーによってスマート化する試み。そのほうが「より管理、整理がしやすく、今後のプランも立てやすい」とマイヤーソン氏。

ここでは、より大規模な「スマートシティ」や、より小規模な「スマートビル」に、中規模な「スマート・プリシンクト」が対置されている。スマートシティは市や政府が関わる規模であり、いち企業が管理できるものではなく調整が困難。かといってスマートビルでは規模が小さすぎ、スマート化による恩恵が小さい。スマート・プリシンクトは、いわば双方の「いいとこどり」なのだ。

スマート・プリシンクトの重要なポリシーとして「インターミックス」というものがある。これは、住宅とオフィス、パブリックとプライベート、バーチャルとリアルなど、異なるコミュニティをつなげることを指す。

そこではデータが収集されるほか、サービスが共用される。「例えば、ミーティングの際の食事をどうして持参しなくてはならないのか。飲食店がたくさんあるプリシンクトに行けばよいのでは？」。サービスの共用は、スペースと時間の効率化にもつながる。

これらを考慮するとスマート・プリシンクトには4つの代表的モデルがある。1つ目はエンタープライズ・モデル。大企業中心で、ワークプレイスの確保が重要になる。そこに商業や娯楽、ホスピタリティ、大学などを付け加えることで、1つのプリシンクトとする。具体的な例として、このスマート・プリシンクトの研究を共同で行った不動産デベロッパー、マーバックが手がけたサウス・イブリー（旧オーストラリア・テクノロジー・パーク）が挙げられる。大企業が集積したエリアにリテール、エンターテインメント、ホスピタリティの機能も充実している。

2つ目はエンポリアム・モデル。ここでは50%をリテールが占める。その例としてマイヤーソン氏はロンドンのウェストフィールド・ストラトフォード・シティを挙げた。「50%が商店で、20%が住宅、20%がワークスペースで、残りが教育や文化の展示場などです」。ショッピングセンターだが大学やオフィスビルの真ん中にあり、ロンドンの国際裁判所も近い。エンターテインメントもあるため多くの人を引き寄せる。そうして商店からリアルタイムの情報を得て、そのデータをもとにプリシンクトを改善している。

「ウェルビーイングやフィットネス、社交なども仕事の一部なのです。皮肉なことに、日本ではこのような多目的の施設を多く開発していますが、その中心にワークスペースを置かず、職場はそこから分けてしまっています」

3つ目はヘイヴェン・モデル。こちらは住宅の割合が多いモデルだ。「ベッドタウンを増やすと地域の雰囲気が暗くなります。寝るためだけのベッドタウンではなく、人々が暮らしを楽しむ地域をつくろうと考えました。そこに根付き、長期的に暮らすことで、いいコミュニティができます。このプリシンクトでは自宅勤務なども可能です」

4つ目はインターチェンジ・モデルだ。これは交通の結節点が中心的な役割を果たす。ロンドンのキングス・クロス駅周辺が好例だ。すべてのビルが駅を中心に立ち並び、インターチェンジから最新のリアルタイム情報がオフィスに流れ込む。

なかでも、理想的なプリシンクトのサイズはどれぐらいなのだろう。

「データベースを効率よく共有するためには、キングス・クロスのような方法がベストだと思います。1,800戸もの住宅があるキングス・クロスだとたくさんの人を引き寄せることができます。小さいですが、理想の結果を出せる大きさです。そのキングス・クロスが大学を含めて67エイカーの広さなので、それが最大だと思います」

スマート・プリシンクトにおいては、オフィスビルのあり方も再定義される。「孤立せず、外につながるための場所」とマイヤーソン氏は言う。そのために、ミーティングルームはより多く、デスクはより少なくなる。

「その方がより人が入りやすく、コミュニケーションを取りやすいからです。伝統的なオフィスの雰囲気は変わりつつあると思います」 **WS**

スマート・プリシンクトの代表的なモデル

1. The Enterprise Model
エンタープライズ・モデル

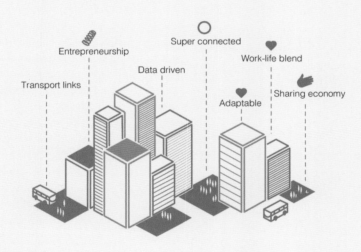

2. The Emporium Model
エンポリアム・モデル

3. The Haven Model
ヘイヴェン・モデル

4. The Interchange Model
インターチェンジ・モデル

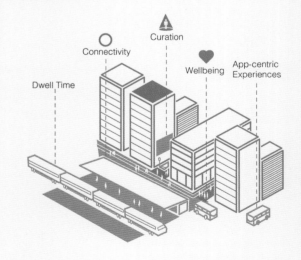

バルセロナ市民に
ストリートを取り戻す

Superblocks

［スーパーブロック］

**Taking back the streets
for Barcelona's citizens**

Superblocks
バルセロナ［スペイン］
実装：2016年から

バルセロナ上空。碁盤目状に整理
されたブロックの様子がよくわかる。
スーパーブロックは複数のブロック
を1つのセットにし、市民生活向上
のために再整備するプロジェクトだ。

©AGE FOTOSTOCK / AFLO

1

2

3

1／スーパーブロックが導入されたポブレノ地区（2〜6も同地区）。交差点だった場所を公園につくり替えた。週末には地区全体でディナーを催すなど、パブリックスペースを存分に活用している。

2／ストリートに設置されたEV（電気自動車）用の充電スタンド。バルセロナでは騒音・大気汚染対策としてEVを積極的に推奨している。

4

5

6

3／陸上のトラックを模したストリートには、キックボードやローラーボードに興じる市民の姿が。交通量が制限されているため、路面に活動できる面積が増加した。

4／公園は遊具を備えた本格的なもので、以前はストリートで見かけなかった子どもたちの姿が見られるようになった。

5／元道路に直接設置されたベンチ。市民同士の会話を育むため、車座に配置されている。

6／スーパーブロック内での自動車の通行は厳しく制限されている。交通量が減り、ゴミ収集車やバスなどの公共交通機関はよりスムーズに業務を進められるように。

ポブレノ地区。植栽やベンチが交差点に大きくせり出している。当初は住宅価格が下がることや不便さを恐れた市民の反感を買ったが、現在は店を構える自動車ディーラーなどを除き、おおむね好意的に受け取られている。

スーパーブロックのつくり方

Conventional Model
従来のモデル

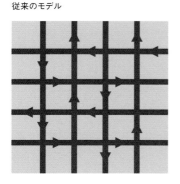

道路は一方通行でスピードも出やすく、騒音と公害が悪影響を及ぼしている。

Superblocks Model
スーパーブロック・モデル

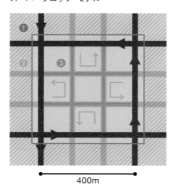

← 400m →

❶ セルダ・プランの隣接する9つのブロックを選ぶ
❷ 内側に走る4本の道路を一方通行から回遊させる
❸ 囲まれた道路部分を市民に向けて再整備する

スーパーブロックの導入ステップ

第3段階
Structural Level
ストラクチュラル・レベル

タクティカル・アーバニズムなどさまざまな実験の成果を踏まえ、街の構造そのものを長期的かつ計画的な工事によって根本的につくり替える。サン・アントニ地区のリニューアルは1つの完成形。

↑

第2段階
Tactical Urbanism
タクティカル・アーバニズム

大きな建設機械を使って道路の形を変えるのではなく、遊具やベンチを置くなど、既存の街を簡易的な手段で変える。道路にペイントを施すだけといった手法も含む。ポブレノ地区はこの段階にあたる。

↑

第1段階
Basic Level
ベーシック・レベル

交通整理のみを行うレベル。自動車が通行できる時間に制限を設けたり、歩行者優先エリアの標識を各道路に整備してブロック内を人々が自由に行き交うことができるようにした段階である。

街は本来、人々のためにある。ここバルセロナの路上にもかつては、食事の準備をはじめ、生活する人々のディテールがあった。しかし世界中の都市がそうであるように、バルセロナも自動車によって埋め尽くされて久しい。

この課題に対してバルセロナ市が提示した解決策が「スーパーブロック」プロジェクトだ。街を市民の手に取り戻し、より健康的に、よりサステナブルに、つまり、よりスマートに街を変える。

仕組みとしてはごくシンプルなものだ。19世紀末に都市計画家イルデフォンソ・セルダが考案した通称「セルダ・プラン」、基本的にはその碁盤の目状に区分けされた複数のブロックを1セットとし、通り抜けできないよう内側の自動車交通を制限する。ブロックの内側は地元住民の自転車と歩行者を主体とし、街並みも住民の意見をもとにつくり替えた。そこには緑があり、公園があり、日々の暮らしを営む市民の姿がある。「スーパーブロックでは、人々と持続可能なモビリティ（自転車と公共交通機関）を優先します。そして、市全体で自動車の21%減を目指しています」（バルセロナ市役所都市環境部門のネダ・コスタンディノビッチ氏）

バルセロナの歴史を振り返れば、スーパーブロックはより意義深いものになる。バルセロナはこれまで3つの大きな変化を経験してきた。スペインの独裁政権が1975年に倒れ、民主主義がもたらされた時代。92年のバルセロナ・オリンピックをホストするにあたり、高速道路ほか重要なインフラが整備された時代。そして92年以降のポストオリンピックの時代。現在に至るまで、バルセロナは変化を続けている。碁盤の目状の市街も、日照性や通気性など市民の快適さを考えて設計されたものだ。だが一方で、バルセロナの生活環境は限界を迎えていた。市民1人に対して10㎡の緑地を割り当てることを推奨しながら実際は1人あたり6.64㎡しかない。ヒートアイランド現象も深刻で、市の中心地と周辺エリアでは気温が4度違う。自動車による騒音や排ガスも、WHOが定める基準値を超えている。

しかしバルセロナに緑地を増やせる余地はない。そこでスーパーブロックなのである。これなら、街の形はそのままに市民の生活の質を改善できる。

スーパーブロックの実装は3つのレベルで行われた。第1の「ベーシック・レベル」は、モビリティの変更が中心。歩行者優先エリアの標識を各道路に整備する、自動車の使用に時間制限を設ける、などだ。第2のレベルは「タクティカル・アーバニズム」と呼ばれる。遊具やベンチ、ペイントなど、取り外し可能で比較的安価なマテリアルを活用する。第3のレベルが「ストラクチュラル・レベル」。大規模な工事を入れ、歩道や道路など街の構造部分からつくり替える段階だ。

ほかのスマートシティと大きく違う点に、「市民参加」がある。都市計画は市民の生活習慣を否応なく変える。「スーパーブロックの実装においては、最初から市民参加プロセスを通じて市民を巻き込みたいと思っています。彼らはこの土地を誰よりも知っているのですから」（同市役所でスーパーブロック・コーディネーターを務めるアリアナ・ミケル氏）。結果的に市民に喜ばれてはいるものの、市民参加のプロセスを省いてタクティカル・アーバニズムを実装したポブレノ地区では、突然起きた変化を前にして市民は激怒したという。これを反省材料に、サン・アントニ地区への実装の際には計画の初期から市民を参加させた。バルセロナ市民は自身の手で、バルセロナの街を取り戻そうとしているのである。 **WS**

スーパーブロックが導入されたサン・アントニ地区。2018年に9年ぶりに改修されたサン・アントニ市場を中心にパブリックエリアが広がる。実装の第3段階に達しており、歩道や道路のストラクチャーを大きくつくり替えている。

スーパーブロックの社会的インパクト

スーパーブロックが現在の6カ所から当初計画通りの503カ所に拡大された場合の社会的インパクトを試算したものである。※Barcelona Institute for Global Health による

Premature deaths
667 PEOPLE

若年での死亡者が667人減少

Ambient levels of NO_2
24%

大気中の二酸化窒素を24%削減

Life expectancy of the average
200 Days

平均寿命が200日分長くなる

バルセロナ市役所
スーパーブロック・コーディネーター
アリアナ・ミケル

Ariadna Miquel
Superblocks Coordinator
Barcelona City Council

バルセロナ市役所
都市環境部門
ネダ・コスタンディノビッチ

Neda Kostandinovic
Urban Ecology
Barcelona City Council

グローバルからローカルへ。
経済活動をボトムアップに変える「ファブシティ」

Fab City

From global to local:
building economic activity from the ground up

IAAC／ファブラボ・バルセロナ
ディレクター
トマス・ディアス

Tomas Diez
Director
IAAC / Fab Lab Barcelona

ベネズエラ出身。社会におけるデジタル
テクノロジーの影響に特化した都市主義
者であり、IAAC（カタルーニャ先進建築
大学院大学）における修士課程、未来デ
ザイン科のディレクター。

1

2

3

4

1／IAACのメイン校舎内。IAAC
は2001年に開設された新時代の
建築を探求するユニークな大学院
大学。校舎内にはプロジェクトの
アウトプットがところ狭しと並ぶ。

2／IAACのファブ・スペース。大
がかりな工作機械が多数並べられ
ており、学生の制作物、プロジェク
トなどに使われる。

3／IAAC内に設けられたファブラ
ボ・バルセロナの執務スペース。

4／IAACメイン校舎の外観。キャ
ンパスは工業地域からイノベーシ
ョン・ディストリクトへと変貌した
ポブレノ（2カ所）とグリーン・ファ
ブラボのある郊外バルダウラ。

PITO to DITO

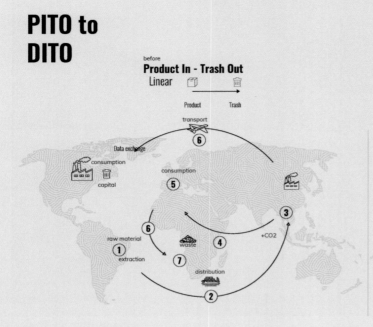

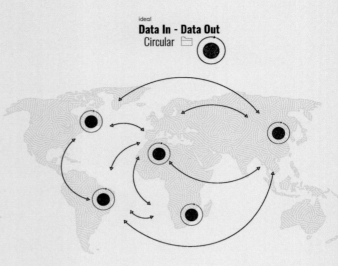

©Tomas Diez in collaboration with Kate Armstrong

左は従来の生産／消費モデルを示したもの。各拠点をリニアにマテリアルが移動していく。右が新しい生産／消費モデル。物流はよりコンパクトになり、行き来するのはデータだけ。

「フ ァブシティ」のコンセプトは「製造のリ・ローカライズ」。ファブラボ・バルセロナのディレクター、トマス・ディアス氏はそう説明する。それは地球規模にまで拡大した生産／消費モデルを、再び地域の手に戻すことであり、食・エネルギー・モノの製造拠点を消費の拠点に近付けることを意味している。

グローバリゼーションは生産、消費、廃棄のすべての拠点を世界各地に分散させる性質を持つ。各拠点間をマテリアルが移動するのに要する化石燃料を考えれば、環境負担は大きい。また「人々をより透明性の低い製造チェーンに依存」させもするとディアス氏は言う。ファブシティはこの構図を反転させるプロジェクトだと言える。

問題は、どうやってこれを実装するか。「スマートシティは都市モデルにICT技術を持ち込むというコンセプトでしたが、問題は実装の点で非常にトップダウンなアプローチを取っていることです」。そのためスマートシティ化で得られるメリットは、市民ではなくテクノロジーを供給する企業側が享受するのみだ。また「政府はスマートシティのアプローチで都市をコントロールしようとしてきました。私はそれを愚かな行為だと思っています」とディアス氏。なぜなら都市は常に変わりゆく。変化することが前提であり、スマートテクノロジーよりもはるかにオーガニックだ。

ファブシティは、より柔軟な分散型コミュニティを通じた実装を試みる。それはボトムアップ型のアプローチだ。世界各地の1,700ものファブラボまたはメイカースペースがインフラとなる。「ファブラボやメイカースペースは人々とつながり、ローカルにインパクトをもたらします」。これまで消費者としての存在だった市民を、クリエイターとして生まれ変わらせる可能性を秘めている。

現に「都市で消費するものを都市で製造する」というアジェンダに共感し、34の都市がファブシティとして名乗りを上げている。これは、ファブラボ周辺のコミュニティがファブシティに参加するよう行政を説得した結果だ。その中には日本の鎌倉市も含まれている。

ただし本格的な実装はこれから。都市スケールで実装するには行政との煩雑な手続きが障壁になることもわかっている。

バルセロナでは、都市よりも小さな「地区」のスケールで「ファブシティ・プロトタイプ」を検証している段階だ。例えばIKEAのオープン・イノベーション・ラボであるSPACE 10とのプロジェクト「Made Again Challenge」を実行している。このチャレンジはファブシティのプロトタイプとしてポブレノ地区を想定するのに役立ち、のちに地元の政策立案者によってメーカー地区としての公共政策となった。

ポブレノでのこれらの取り組みは、ファブラボ・バルセロナとバルセロナ市が作成したファブラボのパブリック・ネットワーク（ファブリケーション・アテナエウム）に含まれている。ほかにも、IAACと共同で郊外に「グリーン・ファブラボ」を設立し、エネルギー、食品、モノの循環型経済の理論化と実践を進めている。

また、パブリックインフラにファブラボを加える都市も生まれている。バルセロナ、サンパウロ、ソウルでも同じことが起きている。

ファブシティのネクストステップはどのような形をとるのか。これまではディアス氏が主宰するIAACやファブラボ・バルセロナなどが主体となってプロジェクトを推し進めてきた。しかし世界各地ではローカルなグループがバラバラに動いている。そこで彼らを、ファブシティに関わるワークショップやリサーチを行う「ファブシティ・コレクティブ」、ファブシティを宣言した都市においてパブリック・セクターとプライベート・セクターをまとめる「ファブシティ・ネットワーク」、そしてファブシティの発展をサポートするファイナンス組織として「ファブシティ・ファウンデーション」を設立し、組織化するという。

「次の目標は、ファブシティ・グローバル・イニシアチブのような複雑なプロジェクトの達成に必要な、さまざまなレベルの補完的な戦略、プログラム、アクション、およびプロジェクトで構成されるファブシティ・フルスタックを開発することです。これにより、ファブアカデミーなどの既存のプログラムやプロジェクトから、大きなビジョンを小さな断片に分解して構築できます。また、ファブシティ・ファウンデーションのようにグローバルに運営できる分散型組織をサポートし、メーカーや技術者以外の幅広いネットワークとの取り組みを調整していきたいと考えています」 WS

RESCALING GLOBAL MANUFACTURING

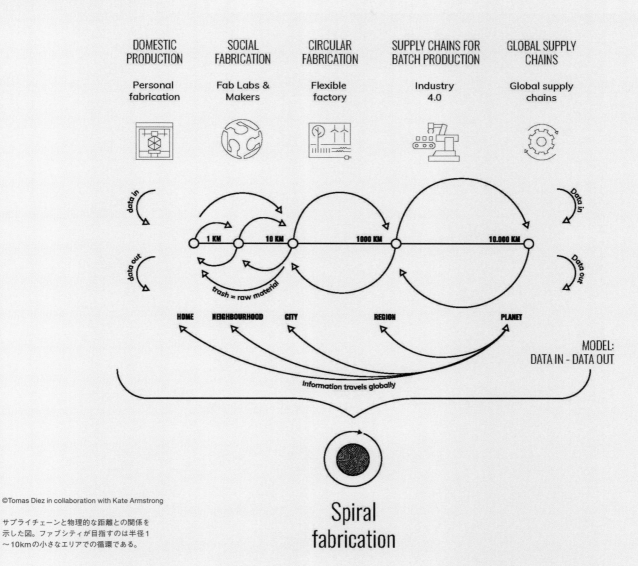

DOMESTIC PRODUCTION	SOCIAL FABRICATION	CIRCULAR FABRICATION	SUPPLY CHAINS FOR BATCH PRODUCTION	GLOBAL SUPPLY CHAINS
Personal fabrication	Fab Labs & Makers	Flexible factory	Industry 4.0	Global supply chains

©Tomas Diez in collaboration with Kate Armstrong

サプライチェーンと物理的な距離との関係を示した図。ファブシティが目指すのは半径1〜10kmの小さなエリアでの循環である。

IAACとファブシティ・ネットワークが推進するプロジェクト「Green Fab Lab（グリーン・ファブラボ）」。21世紀の都市再生のために、自然から直接学ぶ機会を提供している。エネルギー、食品、モノの生産研究所を持ち、世界中の主要な研究センターと連携してプロジェクトと学術プログラムを開発。

バルセロナで行われた「Made Again Challenge」。SPACE 10やIKEAのデザイナー、地元や海外から集まったメイカーたちが参加した。モノの小さな循環をつくるためのトライアル・プロジェクトだ。

FOCUS 5

データの主権を個人に取り戻す
「データ・コモン」

DECODE

The data commons:
Taking back control of our data

ディコード
リサーチャー
パブロ・アラゴン

Pablo Aragón
Researcher
DECODE

データ・サイエンティスト。データ分析を
通じて社会現象・政治現象に焦点を当て
る。草の根民主主義、参加型民主主義な
どの関心からDECODEにもリサーチャ
ーとして参加している。

市民が生み出すデータを大企業が入手し、市民の手の届かないところで管理し、コントロールしている昨今だ。情報社会の中で最も価値の高いものであるはずの個人情報が、市民の手に委ねられていない。スマートシティについてまわる議論である。データは自由に活用し、サービス改善に生かすべきとする議論もあるが、欧州では「個人情報の主権は個人に戻すべき」との意見が主流だ。DECODE（ディコード）はその文脈に位置する。厳格な個人情報保護規制を設けたGDPR（一般データ保護規則）の制約を超えて、個人データをどう社会的に活用していけるか検証するEUのパイロット・プロジェクトだ。現在、バルセロナ、アムステルダムの2都市で大規模な社会実験が進められている。「このプロジェクトの目的は、市民に対して自らが生み出すデータをコントロールできる新たなインフラを供給すること。それからコモン的なやり方でデータを開発・利用することです」とDECODEのリサーチャー、パブロ・アラゴン氏は言う。

一般的には、2つの選択肢が考えられる。1つはプラットフォームで個人データを守る方法。2つ目はオープンソースのように誰もがアクセスできるようネット上でシェアする方法。しかしDECODEはいずれとも異なる3つ目の選択肢として、個人と組織の間に「データ・コモン」をつくろうとしている。データ・コモンはあくまでコミュニティ主導のプラットフォーム。ここに集められたデータはコモン・グッドのために活用され、そのプロセスも市民に対して透明性が保たれる。

バルセロナで行われた実証実験を紹介しよう。1つは個人情報を活用した分散型民主主義のトライアルだ。バルセロナ市役所が開発した参加型民主主義のプラットフォーム「Decidim」をDECODEのインフラに組み込み、市民がDECODEのアプリを通して政策提案できるようにした。なおかつ性別や年齢、住所などの個人情報を条件付きで寄付することが可能になった。従来、個人情報保護の観点から蓄積できなかったデータだが、寄付という形なら集めることができ、人口統計データとして活用できる。もう1つは市民自らがデータをつくるトライアル。騒音データをセンシングするプロセスの中で、市民は個人情報が漏洩する危険に気付き、個人情報保護のルールやプロトコルをつくる動きが見られた。

スマートシティでは、それを管理する自治体や企業が街中にセンサーをちりばめ、データを収集・取得する。対してDECODEは、あくまで市民が主役だ。市民が自らデータを取得、管理し、そこから新しい価値を生み出す。またコモン・グッドな目的から外れることもない。アラゴン氏の言葉を借りるなら、これは「スマートシティからデモクラティックシティへの大きな変換」を推し進める試みなのである。WS

バルセロナでのディコード・パイロット・プロジェクト・ワークショップの様子。©Smart Citizen at Fab Lab Barcelona

参加型民主主義のプラットフォーム「Decidim」

バルセロナ市議会がスタートさせた、都市および組織向けの無料のオープンソース。DECODEと連携することで、人口統計をつくる際に必要な有権者の属性データを匿名で収集できる。

データと市民との関係は
トップダウンからボトムアップへ

Top-down Approach
トップダウン型のアプローチ

Government
政府

DATA

Citizens
市民

Centralization
中央集権化

Bottom-up Approach
ボトムアップ型のアプローチ

Government
政府

DATA

Citizens
市民

Democratization
民主化

条件を満たした市民は、DECODEを通じて個人情報を提供する。これには、どの人口統計グループが政策立案に参加したかなどの貴重な情報が含まれている。

宇宙船「自分」号：
オーナーシップが問われる時代

本誌編集長 山下正太郎

過熱するスマートワークプレイスのムーブメント。
このムーブメントはどこから生まれ、どこへ向かうのだろう。
データによってワークスタイルが最適化される時代に求められることとは？

拡大し続けるデジタルプラットフォーム

ここ数年来、ワークプレイスのシーンを牽引してきた「ウェルビーイング」は一般化し、次のトピックとしてテクノロジーを援用した「スマートワークプレイス」が盛り上がりを見せている。このムーブメントには3つの背景がある。

まず、ユーザーの観点から。Uberがタクシー業界を一変させたように、欧米諸国では急速なデジタルディスラプションによって産業構造が大きく変化している。企業は競争力の原資となるテクノロジーを扱う感覚に優れた若いタレントを求めており、その視線は1980年代以降に生まれたミレニアル世代、2000年代以降に生まれたジェネレーションZたちに注がれている。幼少期からデジタルツールに慣れ親しみ、自分好みのサービスをカスタマイズして楽しむ彼らのための柔軟性の高い職場が求められているのだ。

2点目は、サステナビリティ。経済成長の代償として社会的責任を果たす形で環境配慮をする時代から進み、もはや経済成長と地球環境維持は両立しないという論調が主流だ。例えば、オックスフォード大学のケイト・ラワース氏が「ドーナツ経済学」、マサチューセッツ工科大学（MIT）のエリック・ブリニョルフソン氏はGDPに代わる経済指標として「GDP-B」を提案し、持続的繁栄の在り方を模索する。地球誕生以来、人類による地球環境への影響がその他の環境変化よりも大きい時代として「人新世（Anthropocene）」なる言葉まで生まれており、もはやテクノロジーを積極的に活用しサステナブルなワークプレイスをつくることは、言い訳程度の社会的責任ではなく不可避の社会的義務と言っていいだろう。

3点目は、技術的に実現が容易になった点。これまで思想的にデータ駆動型の社会が模索されてきた一方で、収集から分析までのデータをめぐる技術やコストの問題が解消できなかった。しかしそれもクリアになりつつある。例えばセンサーと通信設備を備えたIoT、そこで取得されたデータが貯められるクラウド、そのビッグデータを分析するAIなど、一連のフローが可能になったのだ。データをめぐるエコシステムが構築されることで「デジタルツイン」と呼ばれる仮想現実で高度なシミュレーションが可能となり、現実世界の空間運用が効率的かつ効果的に行える技術的下地は整った。

こうした背景から進むスマート化だが、どこへ向かっているのだろうか？　古くは1990年代頃から「スマートビル」と呼ばれる環境配慮型のビルが存在してきた。一方、現代の「スマートワークプレイス」は、ワーカーの「エクスペリエンス」を軸にその理想像が模索されている。ラップトップとスマートフォンでいつでもどこでも仕事ができるABWの時代にあって、ワーカーに用意されるオフィス空間は機能的で、ワークとライフがミックスされた体験価値の高いものでなければならない。さらにジェネレーションや国籍など、職場におけるダイバーシティの高まりは留まるところを知らず、彼らワーカーに対してそれぞれに適した体験価値は大きく異なるはずだ。今回取り上げた事例は、スマートフォンのアプリを起点にワーカーの多様なニーズに対して事細かにパーソナライズすることで圧倒的なエクスペリエンスを実現していた。こうしたアプリを中心とした働き方を「APP Centric Work（アプリ中心主義の働き方）」と未来学者フィリップ・ロス氏は名付けている。アプリのみならず、その先に案内される物理的空間もどこにでもあるような間に合わせのものであってはオフィスに来る理由を失ってしまうため、圧倒的なクオリティが求められる。実際にスマート化が進むにつれてオフィスの「アメニティ・リッチ化」がグローバルで進んできている。

山下正太郎
Shotaro Yamashita

コクヨ株式会社 ワークスタイル研究所 所長。次世代ワークプレイスの研究、コンサルティングに従事。2016〜2017年、英ロイヤル・カレッジ・オブ・アート ヘレン・ハムリン・センター・フォー・デザイン客員研究員。

このスマート化のムーブメントは、ユーザー企業ではなく、不動産デベロッパーなどのサプライヤー側から仕掛けられている。ABWは企業のセンターオフィスの面積減に明らかに影響を及ぼす。残された少ない賃貸面積をより高収益化するために、デベロッパーはビルのスマート化に積極的なのだ。ほかにもスマート化を進めるプレーヤーがいる。スマート化は多くのデータを集めれば集めるほど、パーソナライズの精度が上がる。ならばオフィスフロアからビル全体、そして都市へとスマート化の範囲を広げていくことが理にかなっている。Googleがトロントのキーサイド地区で開発を行う「IDEA」などは、まさに都市全体にデジタルプラットフォームの傘をかけ、そこで行われるすべての活動のデータを統合しようとしている。こうしたデジタルプラットフォームの特徴を『Platform Capitalism』の著者ニック・スルニチェック氏は4点挙げている。「1.集団のインタラクションを生むデジタルインフラである」「2.ネットワーク効果を生み、それによって成長する」「3.無料サービスの提供を通じて、ユーザーを集める」「4.ユーザーのエンゲージメントを高め、データをより多く集める」。データが次のデータを生み出し、人やモノの動きがますます最適化されていく。旧来のプレー

ヤーが提供する都市や建築といった物理的プラットフォームを、テックカンパニーが提供するデジタルプラットフォームが覆い隠す時代がもうそこまできている。

デジタル時代に求められるオーナーシップ

デジタルプラットフォームによる利便性の追求の先に、我々には何が待っているのだろうか？
残念ながら、先述したようにスマート化はサプライヤー主導で進められているからであろう、消費を刺激するレコメンド経済以外に未来像が見えていないのが現状だ。経済学者でありアナーキストのデヴィッド・グレーバー氏はその著書『官僚制のユートピア』『Bullshit Jobs』の中で、官僚制が仕事を細分化、無限に無味乾燥な内容を生み出しワーカーがそこに隷属させられる実情を鮮やかに描いている。現代人の仕事に対する低いエンゲージメントは社会問題となっており、人間が生み出したシステムが社会を覆い、人間をパーツの一部として機能させることで、生気を失わせる。この構造はデジタルプラットフォーム社会のそれと正に酷似する。
つまるところ、これからのデータ社会の方向性を考える上で、私たちは「便利／安心」と「自

由／挑戦」を天秤にかけていると言える。多くの個人データを提供する代わりに、無駄なく、迷うことなく自分に適したサービスを受けられる一方で、多少の失敗は織り込んだ上でのセレンディビティや生活の機微を失うことにもつながりかねない。よほど自分の生き方に強い「オーナーシップ」を持っていない限り、データの海の中で泳がされる可能性が高い。今回取り上げたスーパーブロック、DECODEは欧州の強い個人主義を背景にして、この社会変化に対していち早くNOを突きつけ、データの主権を取り戻し、自らの生き方や働き方にオーナーシップを持つことを主題にしている。
スマートワークプレイスを生かすも殺すも、自らが生き方や働き方にオーナーシップを持っているかどうかにかかっている。20世紀に建築、化学、エコロジー思想など、横断的な分野で活躍した偉大なテックシンカーであるバックミンスター・フラー氏は、境目のない地球を1つのシステムと捉え、人類は宇宙船地球号の乗組員と考えるべきだと説いた。ワークとライフ、このどこまでも（それこそ宇宙まで！）フラットにデジタル化された世界を、「自分」という宇宙船はどこへ進むべきなのか。操縦桿を握るのはデータではなく、あなたであるべきではないだろうか？ **WS**

DATA SHEET

[データシート]

The Edge
コンサルティング（ワークスタイル）：非公開
建築設計：PLP Architecture
インテリア設計：Fokkema & Partners
Consultancy for Work Style: N/A
Architect: PLP Architecture
Interior Design: Fokkema & Partners

Edge Olympic Amsterdam
コンサルティング（ワークスタイル）：非公開
建築設計：de Architecten CIE.
インテリア設計：Concrete
Consultancy for Work Style: N/A
Architect: de Architecten CIE.
Interior Design: Concrete

22 Bishopsgate
コンサルティング（ワークスタイル）：非公開
建築設計：PLP Architecture
インテリア設計：PLP Architectureとその他のデザイン・カンパニー
Consultancy for Work Style: N/A
Architect: PLP Architecture
Interior Design: PLP Architecture and the other design companies

Microsoft Netherlands
コンサルティング（ワークスタイル）：D/DOCK
建築設計：D/DOCK
インテリア設計：D/DOCK
Consultancy for Work Style: D/DOCK
Architect: D/DOCK
Interior Design: D/DOCK

CIRCL
コンサルティング（ワークスタイル）：非公開
建築設計：Cie Architects
インテリア設計：Doepelstrijkers
Consultancy for Work Style: N/A
Architect: Cie Architects
Interior Design: Doepelstrijkers

B. Amsterdam
コンサルティング（ワークスタイル）：非公開
建築設計：N/A
インテリア設計：N/A
Consultancy for Work Style: N/A
Architect: N/A
Interior Design: N/A

EDITORS' NOTE

[編集後記]

意 外にも取材した人みながヒューマニストだった。彼らから、スマートとはテクノロジーではなく理想的な働き方を実現するための「アティチュード」なのだと教わった。スマートフォンから日々レコメンドされる情報に埋もれながら、自分にとっての理想を改めて考えてみたいと思った次第。（山下）

「スマート」何々というとテクノロジーを活用して利便性を高めるイメージが強いが、実際の解釈のされ方はさまざまだ。スペース効率を高める運用方法、既存のルールにとらわれないスペースの使い方や働き方、明確な目的のために意志をもってつくられた空間など、テクノロジーはキーワードだが進化の余地はまだまだありそうだ。（金森）

Everyone interviewed for this issue, surprisingly enough, is a humanist. They taught us that smart is less about technology, and more about attitude—one that will bring about the best, most ideal ways to work. While struggling to stay on top of the daily deluge of information recommended by my smartphone, I find myself inspired to rethink my own ideals anew.
—— Shotaro Yamashita

We tend to think of "smart" as technology that makes our lives more convenient, but there are many ways to interpret what it means. Sure tech can be used operationally in the workplace to maximize space efficiency, to enable new ways to work untethered from conventional rules, to design intentional spaces for specific purposes, but really tech is more of a keyword in the grander scheme of progress in which "smart" can take many different forms.
—— Yuki Kanamori

NEXT ISSUE WORKSIGHT 16号

[次号予告]

スマートワークプレイス特集 第2弾

世界で最もフレキシブルな働き方を実践するオーストラリア。ABW、ウェルビーイングはもちろんワーカーファーストのテクノロジー、サーキュラー・エコノミーなど、ワーカーにも地球にもサステナブルな進化し続けるワークプレイスに迫る。

www.worksight.jp

The Edge

The Edge
Amsterdam [The Netherlands]
Completion: 2014
Total area: Approximately 40,000㎡

Each floor opens up to the atrium in the center of the building, allowing employees to be visible to one another. The space impacts a feeling that the building is alive.

A pioneering smart building that cultivates "experiences"

The building The Edge—known as the first to introduce technology that enhances employee experience in real time—paved the way for a new era of smart buildings that went beyond the conventional idea that "smart" simply means "sustainable." Finding available workspaces, looking up the whereabouts of colleagues, unlocking lockers and doors, all suddenly became accessible through a user-friendly app. The Edge thus became one of the first buildings to embrace the app-centric workplace, changing the way employees work.

Although The Edge is a tenant-leased building, because 60% is occupied by the firm Deloitte, the general appearance and design caters to the Deloitte brand. In fact, the aforementioned building app, which all tenants can access, was the product of a collaboration between Deloitte and the Delft University of Technology that produced the startup Mapiq. Also notable is that the app is a mashup of several systems developed by a number of tenant startups, and

that the building's software is continuously being updated, earning it the nickname: the "computer with a roof."

What really defines The Edge as the world's smartest building, though, is its strength in four key areas: sustainability, well-being, smart technology, and social interactivity.

Starting with sustainability, Europe's leading sustainability assessment method BREEAM gives it an environmental performance score of 98.4%, the highest in the

world. There are several reasons for this. First, the atrium is north-facing so the building is less impacted by direct sunlight, allowing for a larger opening in the facade. In addition, it's strategic interior layout allows sunlight to reach an impressive 70% of desk space. And the incorporation of renewable energy, including an electric thermal storage heater that uses the aquifer 130 meters below ground to store warm water during the summer for use in the winter, saves the building a massive amount of energy.

The Edge is also dedicated to maximizing the well-being of its users. The abundant natural light throughout the building promotes a sense of optimism, enhancing productivity and creativity. The app also enables each employee to adjust lighting and temperature to their liking, and there's a beautiful in-house restaurant serving locally sourced fresh ingredients.

Space utilization is also extremely efficient. The initial design allocated 3,100 desk spaces for each of the 3,100 Deloitte employees in a 50,000㎡ area, but the collapse of Lehman Brothers triggered a rebalancing of cost and space. The new design accommodates 1,000 desks for the 3,100 employees in a total area of 40,000㎡, and although on paper that means less space per employee, it also allows for the flexibility of activity-based working(ABW). The workspace now offers a choice of desks, sofas, standing desks, booths, and so on, to accommodate different preferences, and the building's abundant amenities including a deluxe fitness room are nothing short of impressive.

The Edge's app and the app-centric work it enables are both products of smart technology. "A lot of people who talk about smart buildings talk about energy...but [that's] only a very small portion of it," says Erik Ubels, who came on board during the planning phase as the point person from Deloitte, and is now the CTO of EDGE, a real estate developer previously known as OVG Real Estate. That's because the true objective of smart technology is to be smart—to help cut down on things like cleaning and maintenance costs, while also increasing user satisfaction, productivity, and experience.

What makes this smart tech possible are the four types of 28,000 sensors installed in the ceiling. Everything from the location of employees to the status of each of the coffee machines, which are managed by a catering company located on a lower floor, is IoT enabled. Are the machines clean, do they have enough milk, what about coffee beans? In other words, knowing the current status of the machines means eliminating unnecessary labor and maintenance. Likewise, power can be shut off as needed on unoccupied floors, and unused bathrooms do not need to be flagged for cleaning.

"If you run to a coffee machine and it doesn't work, you're not happy. If the copier doesn't work, you're not happy. If the toilets are not clean, you're not happy," explains Ubels. "You use sensors [to see] how is the building being used, how can

1. The second floor lounge. Although it is an open space, sound absorbent floors keep noise from travelling. Finishes are kept minimal to dampen the effect of sound bouncing off surfaces.
2. A Deloitte event space near the top floor. The coffee machines are IoT enabled to optimize their maintenance.
3. The building exterior. Lined with solar panels, the roof is tilted at 22 degrees toward the sun.
4. The large atrium plays an important role in energy efficiency. The structure enables heat distribution from the atrium to reach other areas of the building without the need for ventilation systems.

we optimize it? From energy, from cleaning, from making you happy, productive, et cetera."

The final component of smart technology is to promote the kind of social interactions that connect people. Ubels believes that what enables this is the integration of smart technology, sustainability, and well-being. For example, take the enormous atrium: though at first glance it seems like an indulgent use of space, it's actually serving as a massive energy-efficient chimney, sending heat out to every corner of the building. "With this atrium, where you can see all the different people working, you feel a vibe, you feel the building is alive," notes Ubels. "[It's] completely different than in a traditional building where you go in, and maybe you go to the 60th floor, and you have no idea what your colleagues are doing or what's going on on the other floors, [but] this makes it more like a living organization. And even if you do not talk to your colleagues directly during the day but you're just seeing them, you feel that you are part of a company, and you're part of something. ...people really like the effect of that."

So how does Deloitte benefit from being headquartered in this smart building? One way is by attracting top talent and keeping the company competitive as an attractive place to work, in a global recruiting climate where hiring good employees is a major factor in determining the success of a company. Starting with millenials, the younger generation is looking for work environments that are positive, that promote good productivity and high levels of job satisfaction, and that are environmentally conscious. In other words, wanting to spend time in a specific space is a major factor in choosing where to work.

In that sense, The Edge exceeds the expectations of the younger generation. Deloitte now receives 2.5 times the number of applications, employee absences are down by 45%, and productivity has increased. Compared to conventional buildings, maintenance fees are 40% lower, and electricity costs 70% less. In an astonishingly short five years since completion, The Edge has already demonstrated the enormous impact that smart buildings can achieve. **WS**

©Ronald Tileman ©Horizon Photoworks ©Ronald Tileman ©Horizon Photoworks ©Raimond Wouda ©Horizon Photoworks ©Horizon Photoworks ©Horizon Photoworks

An in-house app facilitates interactivity

The collaborative app between Deloitte and Delft University of Technology. Each new technology introduced to the building is made accessible via this app, anything from reserving a workspace, to adjusting lighting and room temperature, down to recording exercise history.

Central management of information

The 28,000 sensors installed in the ceiling collect data throughout the building. A dashboard shows facility information such as frequency of use, electricity consumption, temperature, and projected productivity.

The Edge's quantitative achievements

SMART TECHNOLOGY	SUSTAINABILITY	WELLBEING
BUILDING MANAGEMENT COST	**ELECTRICITY COST**	**ABSENTEEISM**
40% ↘	70% ↘	45% ↘
CAPITAL COST RETURN	**HEATING AND COOLING COST**	**EMPLOYEE SATISFACTION**
8.3 YEARS	±0	UP ↗
SPACE OPTIMIZATION	**CARBON NEUTRALITY**	**TALENT ACQUISITION / RISE OF DELOITTE APPLICATIONS**
1,000 DESKS FOR 3,100	±0	2.5x

Edge Olympic Amsterdam

**A flexible smart building that
caters to the individual**

Edge Olympic Amsterdam
Amsterdam [The Netherlands]
Completion: 2018
Total area: 12,367㎡

Located in Amsterdam, and made by the same developers and management companies, Edge Olympic Amsterdam and The Edge (page 81) are like siblings: The Edge is the original pioneer, while the younger Edge Olympic is at the forefront of the smart buildings industry.

The technology used in each has a lot in common. Control of lighting and air conditioning, conference room reservations, all are consolidated on an app. Building details, down to each coffee machine, are IoT enabled, and data is collected from all areas of both buildings. The app's dashboard displays information such as the building's energy consumption, CO2 emissions, noise and light levels. For example, pointing to a number on the dashboard that indicates projected employee productivity, Edge CTO Erik Ubles says, "Overall today, at the moment, it's 94.4 percent." Of course, the data is not absolute, but when building information is visible in this way, employees are likely to be more mindful of productivity. Unlike its older counterpart, the tenant-occupied Edge Olympic is in an existing building that was renovated to retrofit some of the

The central atrium. Occupants include coworking spaces, studios, subtenants on designated floors, and the developer EDGE. The central staircase serves as an ecosystem that connects different users, creating opportunities for unexpected interactions. There are water refilling stations on every floor (seen in right foreground), an amenity that makes sense in environmentally-aware Netherlands.

A communal work lounge on the ground floor. Whether an employee is looking for inspiration, relaxation, or collaboration, a variety of spaces are available to suit different needs.

smartest systems available. This demonstrates that smart is not exclusive to large corporations with limitless capital resources, but can be done with more modest budgets as well.

The building was developed by EDGE, which was previously known as OVG Real Estate. Edge Olympic attracted considerable attention right from the start. What does a building need to enhance the productivity, creativity, and happiness of its occupants? Many anticipated that the building would showcase the newest solutions to such questions.

The results are now in. Instead of being a conventional space designed to control the behaviour of its occupants, Edge Olympic can anticipate and meet the needs of its occupants halfway. As Ubels explains, this is because it has cleared all four stages of becoming a true smart building.

The first stage is to implement data transparency. Edge Olympic achieves this through a dashboard that displays various data from all areas of the building, and by enabling users to adjust the room temperature, lighting, and other aspects of the environment through a proprietary app.

The second stage is to grasp how various data points connect to other data points. For example, knowing the details of a planned meeting with an important client could enhance the client's experience by securing their access to the elevators in advance. Or one could discover what makes one conference room preferable over another for a variety of uses by looking at corresponding data. "Most people on the floor will know, that's a bad meeting room because it's always too warm, too noisy, too whatever... Why do people not change that? That's strange. You're in the building, you pay for it, and people seem to accept that. We want to change that," Ubels says. When there's no data transparency, it's hard to find proof that a certain room is too hot or too noisy, which makes it difficult to identify problems and make improvements.

The third stage of a true smart building is to be aware of usage. How many people are using the room, and in what way? This may seem like a simple matter, but it can become complicated—for example, a sensor might flag a seat with someone's bag on it as being empty, while a person can easily see that it is in fact occupied. At Edge Olympic, the system makes an informed decision through the

1. A coworking space on the third floor. The ceilings are lined with copper pipes to regulate room temperature. In the summertime, cold water is pumped through the pipes from deep underground to absorb excess heat from the building.
2. A meeting space adjacent to the atrium in another tenant coworking space. The biophilic design floods the space with green and camouflages the technology. White noise is used to absorb excess noise.
3. An eatery offering healthy meals is part of the building's wellbeing initiative. The theatrics of the open kitchen stimulates the appetite.
4. A conference room within a coworking space. Users can order coffee or make changes to the room through a voice-activated device.
5. Data showing how many employees used which spaces within a given timeframe, making more and less utilized areas instantly visible.

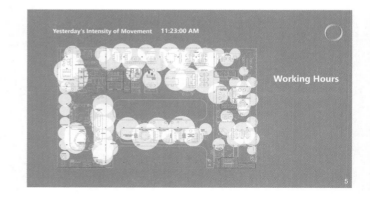

use of thermographic cameras and sensors.

The fourth and final stage is machine learning, where data from the first three stages are consolidated to extract an algorithm. Edge Olympic is at this fourth stage. Like The Edge, the building's system is served by sensors lining the ceilings and furniture, but with 10 different types of devices collecting all kinds of data from 65,000 sensors, Edge Olympic has more than twice as many devices as its predecessor. The collected data is then used to perform a simulation on a digital twin in a virtual space, and finally, the feedback is projected back into the real world. In this way, the building can autonomously guide itself toward optimizing employee activity, energy use, maintenance, cleaning, and so forth. In other words, the building learns how to cater to the needs of its occupants in real time, and has the intelligence to execute those changes. This is what makes Edge Olympic one of the world's smartest buildings, and the reason why there are numerous "Edge" brand projects in progress around the world. The day that The Edge becomes synonymous with the concept of smart buildings itself might not be so far into the future. **WS**

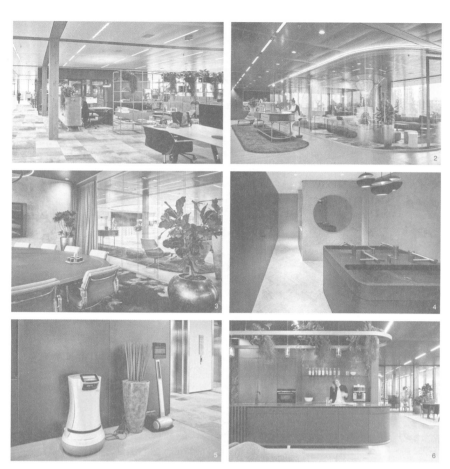

Erik Ubels
CTO
EDGE

1. A floor occupied by the building's developer, EDGE. Two floors with a wood-frame structure were added to the original building. Together with the homey furniture, the space is designed to create a healthy atmosphere.
2. The reception area. A good example of technology replacing the need for a formal reception lobby.
3. The conference room, equipped with a voice-activated system that can assist with setting up an online conference upon request.
4. A chic and streamlined gender-inclusive bathroom with unisex private stalls.
5. Information robots roam the floor.
6. The cafe area. The coffee machines are equipped with sensors, monitoring how many cups are brewed, whether enough beans are stocked, and if machines are running smoothly. Real-time information eliminates the need for unnecessary maintenance.

The four stages of data utilization

Stage 4:
Machine Learning

↑

Stage 3:
Usage Analysis

↑

Stage 2:
Data Correlation

↑

Stage 1
Data Transparency

Types of Sensors

CO2 · Temperature · Noise · Daylight · PM10 · PM2.5 · Bluetooth localization · Volatile organic compounds · Humidity · Presence

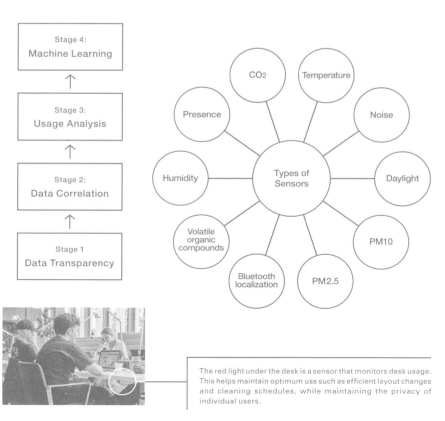

The red light under the desk is a sensor that monitors desk usage. This helps maintain optimum use such as efficient layout changes and cleaning schedules, while maintaining the privacy of individual users.

1. The entrance. A small reception and cafe are placed just inside, creating a welcoming space. Smart technology enables the reception to perform a concierge-like role rather than as a gatekeeper.
2. The reception area of the coworking company Epicenter, known across Europe as a startup incubator.
3. A tiered theater area on the ground floor is used as a common space for the whole building. Available as a leased space, at the time of our visit it was being used by a university program.
4. Lockers within the building can be located and opened through the proprietary building app.
5. Exterior of Edge Olympic, located near the 1928 Amsterdam Olympic Stadium in a quiet area away from the busy city center. The two levels of wood-framed floors added atop the original building are clearly visible.

CASE 2

22 Bishopsgate

A vertical village that blends in with the City of London

City of London, the center of London's Financial District. A new landmark, 22 Bishopsgate, is currently under construction, designed by the same firm as The Edge, PLP Architecture. As many of their previous projects, this design is intended to embody the future of multi-tenant buildings with the underlying idea of a "Vertical Village with amenity share," a new approach to service offerings.

"To create a community, tenants don't want to have to put ammenities into their own space," says Philip Ross, a futurist and CEO of the management consultancy UnWork, who worked on the concept phase. To accommodate, the building features a 10,000㎡ shared amenity space within a total area of 120,000㎡. A coworking space, a club. A gym that includes a climbing wall and high-altitude training room. The Retreat, a space to relax the body and mind. And a restaurant that prepares three-course meals every breakfast, lunch and dinner, with a changing menu that won't bore daily users. "I can't think of another multi-tenanted office building in the world that's got that kind of scale of provision. And I think that's what's a first, which is going to be very exciting, that you have people who can see this as a kind of a home in effect, as a place to do business and also have the ability to exercise, eat, socialize, relax, et cetera," says Ross.

Amenity sharing is increasingly resonating with users, starting with the younger generation. 22 Bishopsgate incorporated the idea of the sharing economy to this multi-tenant building as part of their effort to appeal to millenials and beyond. Then there are the SMEs (small businesses). Abundant amenities are often only available at a selection of large corporations, and has become a major factor in attracting talent. Having access

22 Bishopsgate
London [England]
Scheduled completion date: 2020
Total area: Approximately 120,000㎡

62 floors, 278m high. Nestled among skyscrapers in the heart of London's financial district in the City of London, the polyhedron structure is designed to blend into its surroundings rather than call attention to itself as an icon, in keeping with the building's community-conscious mindset. Scheduled completion date, summer 2020.

A Vertical Village containing four buildings stacked atop the others is equipped with amenity floors shared by all tenants, and stocked with plenty of high-quality options. All building services can be accessed via a proprietary app.

Levels 58 - 61

RESTAURANT, BAR AND VIEWING GALLERY

The publicly accessible Viewing Gallery with panoramic views of the city, as well as a 24-hour restaurant.

Level 41

THE RETREAT

A wellness space for mind and body. Future tenants include a yoga studio, hospital, and dental clinic.

Level 7

THE EXCHANGE

A coworking space where workers can mingle. Desk space is available at discounted rates to support startups. Facilities include a professional recording studio and conference rooms.

Level G

Lobby

In addition to the reception area, there's also a gallery with biannual exhibitions. The basement will accommodate parking for 1,700 bikes and other amenities for the cycling community, such as a bike park.

Level 57

THE CLUB

A high-end business lounge, slated to house private dining and conferences.

Level 25

THE GYM

Equipped with high-end training equipment and a climbing wall, as well as a dance studio. There are different price points depending on level of service used.

Level 2

THE MARKET

A floor-wide food hall with a terrace. Offerings will rotate, including to-go items like sandwiches, as well as three-course meals and pop-up restaurants.

to shared amenities, however, means smaller companies can be competitive recruiters, and by having small businesses as tenants, the building benefits from the buzz of bringing a diversity of values to the city.

The developers began with a vision of building a vertical village. The idea was, stack up four buildings with amenity floors between each building, and create a community where 12,000 people can move and work fluidly. The building would also include spaces open to the public.

"The idea of bringing more amenities and even bringing the public realm into the building became not only a desire of the client but even a mandate from the City," says PLP founding partner Karen Cook. The number of commuters in the central area of the City of London has increased by 100,000 workers over the past 10 years, and the growth shows no sign of stopping. On the planning side, this growth was treated as a logistical problem to improve quality of life, an important factor to a new generation of workers. Cook says that "people want to be with other people. I think technology allows us to work at home, but in fact I think mental health issues are worse because people have become isolated. People want the stimulation of being around other people, and companies want people to be together at work." Taking this into account, she began working on new ideas for the workplace that could responsibly accommodate the growing number of workers, cars, and bicycles in an urban environment. "The answers were interesting from an architectural viewpoint, because it increased the desire to have better social environments."

In short, the building aims to fold seamlessly into the City of London. In an area where skyscrapers vie for attention, it's multifaceted, understated appearance was part of the intention to have a quiet presence, while also being a place where the public can visit the observation deck: "[it] should be a good way for the general public not only in the building, but in the City and in London, and outside of London from across the UK or across the world to come and experience being in the City, and being in the tall building," Cook explains.

This makes 22 Bishopsgate a responsive building in the urban landscape that in many ways favors social responsibility over convenience. For example, there's the consolidated delivery initiative that aims to reduce the number of vehicles in the city, and bring people out to the streets. All deliveries are transported to warehouses outside the city, then delivered in small low-emission vehicles that travel between the warehouse and the building. According to developer Paul Hargraves of Lipton Rogers Developments, "A building of this size could have anything up to a thousand deliveries a day to it, and it reduces it down to 30 deliveries a day."

The roadmap for the building tech is drawn from the latest research of on global smart buildings. A level 1 building considers energy and financial efficiency. Level 2 allows for individualization and optimization for the individual worker, such as workspace customization and room temperature. Level 3 is contextualization, where data gathered from the building provides proposals to tenants on how best to optimize working methods and workflow. Level 4 brings in suggestions based on our 24-hour biological rhythm, such as the need to incorporate time for contemplation, or get some sunlight. Level 5 is the optimization of the building itself by utilizing big data. A true smart building is one that has achieved this level of overarching optimization. "I think nobody's yet a level 5. I'm not sure the technology's yet there [...] I think we're certainly a 3," says Hargreaves. He's looking forward to the building reaching level 5 in the future, when the technology arrives. **WS**

A rendering of the workspace. The interior stairway can be opened up as requested. The multifaceted facade and high-efficiency glass brings in plenty of natural light to promote well-being.

Flexible floorplan

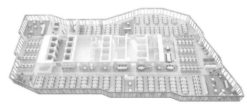

Accommodating up to four tenants on each floor, the design can be customized for a variety of uses. The approach encourages occupancy of smaller businesses over anchor tenants.

Evolution of the Smart Building

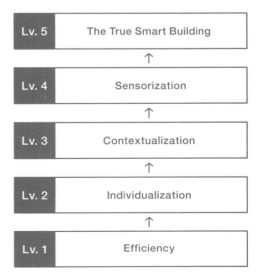

Lv. 5	The True Smart Building
Lv. 4	Sensorization
Lv. 3	Contextualization
Lv. 2	Individualization
Lv. 1	Efficiency

Philip Ross
CEO
UnWork

Paul Hargreaves
Construction Director
Lipton Rogers Developments

Karen Cook
Founding Partner
PLP Architecture

1. At Exchange, the coworking space on the 7th floor, programming will include seminars, courses, and events. The space provides ample places to learn and share new ideas.

2. The ground floor features an inviting and open pedestrian-friendly space. Visitors are greeted with curated paintings and sculptures at the four entrances.

3. The food hall. Open kitchens, food kiosks, restaurants and a terrace bar give plenty of options for dining, meeting, and relaxing. There's also a casual speakeasy for meeting up with friends.

4. Entrance facing Crosby Square. Landscaped greenery and stone paving creates an appealing space.

5. The reception area, originally designed to be a place to linger with artwork and a library, now also fulfills a concierge-like role. Workers can enter via face recognition, and visitors are sent electronic passes for access, greeted by Rooming Concierges.

6. The main entrance facing bustling Bishopsgate Street. The open design is a good fit for a building designed to welcome the general public with a free observatory and 24-hour restaurant. The defining feature is an open canopy that protects from the wind and houses public artworks.

7. A proprietary app allows for workplace customization, including the opening and closing of blinds. Meals from the dining floor can also be ordered directly to each floor.

FOCUS 1

How technology x people will change the future of smart buildings

PLP Architecture

Lee Polisano
Founding Partner & President
PLP Architecture

UK- and US-registered architect. Founder of PLP Architecture, he has worked on more than 40 high-rise and high-rise tower projects. Many are sustainable, have excellent environmental performance, and are highly regarded internationally.

PLP Architecture is known for being a pioneer of smart buildings including The Edge and 22 Bishopsgate. We asked about PLP's past office projects, and what they anticipate for the future.

The firm was founded 10 years ago by Lee Polisano and several co-partners, all originally from the global design office KPF (Kohn Pedersen Fox). After leaving to pursue a different philosophical approach at PLP, they have been collaborating with cities, rethinking how public spaces should be used, and creating spaces where people gather. As Polisano sees it, "We think it's particularly relevant because we believe in the principle that no great innovation or idea or relationship is possible without two people having a conversation with each other." And if you can design a building that enables better communication between people, you can contribute positively to communities of the world at large.

PLP also designed the Crick Institute, a place that's said to have advanced medical research by 20 years. This year the Crick Institute produced another Nobel prize winner in Physiology or Medicine, Peter Ratcliffe. The facility houses 1,250 employees, including Nobel Prize-class researchers, to conduct new cancer research. Here also, the aim of the design was to enhance communication between its inhabitants.

A well-known characteristic of PLP's projects is that each is based on extensive research—the city, culture, building occupants, and technology options—and that concepts are developed accordingly. "It's a slight rethinking of the role of an architect," Polisano says. An architect usually takes a coordinating role between experts in different fields, but as he sees it, "architects are the natural sort of people to [...] make an evolution as to how he or she contributes to society and the future. And there's a danger that if people with a more humanistic approach don't start to participate, people with a highly technological and systematic approach will begin to dominate the way society functions."

In other words, Polisano is interested in focusing on the people who will inhabit the building, rather than on a specific technology: when designing a smart building, he puts people in the center. Take a smart building like The Edge: even with the technology removed, it still functions as a beautiful building, a place where workers meet and create unexpected interactions. And when you combine the building and the technology with the special concepts behind them, it expands the possibilities of both. "We're

1. PLP Architecture is an architectural design office based in London, known for building next-generation smart buildings. A canopy of white light spans the central hallway of the office.
2. The main work area of the PLP office, where employees sit along long desks in the open office.
3. A meeting area in-between individual workspaces. Experts from various fields collaborate on new architectural innovations for the city.
4. The PLP headquarters. Surprisingly for a design office known for their smart buildings, they are housed in a classic Art Deco building in London. About 150 employees occupy one floor.

able to understand that. Because we have an understanding of the power of technology, and we have a great understanding of space, but we also now have an understanding of the combination of the two." His focus is on sustainable building both in the sense of maximized environmental efficiency, as well as a place designed to maximize work happiness by considering the well-being of the occupants.

PLP's approach to research is collaborative rather than passive, working directly with experts at the top of their fields. Their PLP Labs received recognition for OakwoodTimber Tower 2, a proposal for a 130m skyscraper made with the renewable resource of wood, a collaborative project with the Natural Materials Innovation Center at the University of Cambridge. And PLP just won the international competition for a 140m timber hybrid building in Rotterdam which is aiming for a carbon zero tower.

So what direction is PLP headed in the future? As smart buildings gain popularity, the field will undoubtedly become more competitive for design offices, but as Polisano explains, "We don't spend a lot of time thinking about how we can beat our competition. It's not productive time. We have to spend time thinking about how we can be different than others and how we can also have fun doing what we're doing. So we're spending time thinking about what makes us as a group intellectually stronger, and able to deal with what we see as a big big change in the problems of the world that we have to deal with in the built environment."

Having said that, one move they made to help expand their horizons was to open an office in Japan. The reason being, Polisano says, "the society there is very interested in ideas and matured enough to use research to inform the next generation of products or ideas. So we felt by having a presence there we could contribute, and we could also benefit from learning." **WS**

©PLP Architecture

©PLP Architecture

©PLP Architecture

©PLP Architecture

5. The NuMo research project. A proposal for a zero emission, autonomous on-demand mass transportation system.
6. CarTube proposes a dedicated underground tunnel for self-driving cars that would open up more space for pedestrians in urban environments.
7. The SkyPod project looks into the possibility of vertical transport in skyscrapers. Linear motor technology on the exterior of the building powers movement in all directions in the interior.
8. The Oakwood Timber Tower 2. A project exploring the possibilities of wooden high-rise buildings in collaboration with the Natural Materials Innovation Center at the University of Cambridge.
9. Crick Institute, a global cancer research facility in Kings Cross, London. Transparency was an important character of the design to encourage communication between researchers.

PLP Architecture's vision for the smart building of the future

Ron Bakker
Founding Partner
PLP Architecture

Co-founder of PLP architecture. An expert on the role of technology in architecture and its impact on cities. Lecturer at universities and digital technology forums in architecture, including real estate, urban development and TEDx.

Midori Ainoura
Partner
PLP Architecture

20+ years of experience in the UK, US, Europe, Middle East and Asia designing offices, homes, schools and master planning projects. Lead designer of the smart building The Edge in Amsterdam.

The evolution of the value system around "Smart"

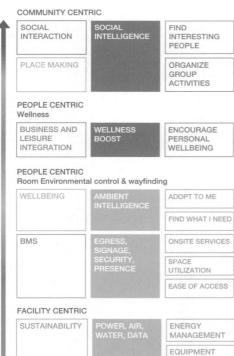

The term "smart" used to refer only to digital technology. Nowadays, "smart" refers to improvements to the workplace in every possible way, meaning all the facilities that help people work better. That's the approach of PLP Founding Partner Ron Bakker.

That means the way smart buildings are made will continue to evolve. "Five years ago, workspace was comfort and sustainability and good air and some technology, but now workspace is also neuroscience, it's social science, how do people work together, and it's also about change of work that we are seeing. [...] it's discussion and communication and collaboration," Bakker explains. The future of smart buildings will incorporate these ongoing changes in how people work. With digital methods replacing manual, the workplace is increasingly centered around creativity and collaboration between people, rather than on more siloed, specialized methods of working. "Office space is more and more for people and less and less for work, or traditional work."

This is where technology comes back into the picture. Sensors can measure things like carbon dioxide levels, room temperature, and electric and natural light—but what do you do with the data? Successfully answering that question can lead to a better, happier workplace. As Bakker explains, "In a really smart building you don't just measure conditions, you also try and understand the relationship between the conditions and the quality of the work and the happiness of the people."

For example, "If there's too much carbon dioxide in the room, people get a headache and slow down. We know that already, so it's good to measure and then you can adjust it. We think we know that daylight is beneficial for people, and it is for most people, but not for all people. There are people who are stressed by daylight, and it's better for them to sit in a dark room for instance. So I think once we're starting to understand conditions better by technology, and we're starting to understand people better, then we can overlap and we can create much better spaces. So I think that's the future."

Is it possible to design buildings that are healthier for everyone? "It's a good question. And the answer is, you don't. You can't make one space that's good for everybody." To create a building that considers the needs of a variety of people, you create a variety of spaces to accommodate.

This type of workplace will become more common, where people can choose between, for example, a more livelier space to work, or a quieter space, depending on their preference and their preferred micro climate.

"It's crazy not to, you know, because people are the most expensive part of the work, for a company. Not if you're making cars, but if you're in the office environment the people are the biggest money. It's much more expensive than the rent or the furniture or the technology or the food or the coffee, the people themselves are the most expensive, and the most important."

When the Imperial College of London studied the factors that affect well-being, they found that the thing had the potential to make people the most unhappy was work—all the more reason to build better workplaces. And the thing that had the most potential to increase well-being and productivity was engagement: whether you felt part of a group, and were a valued member of it. In other words, Bakker says, "If people are very interested in what they're doing, or excited about what they're doing, they work much better." The workspace itself, the quality of the architecture, and location, all these are factors in creating satisfaction. PLP Partner Midori Ainoura tells us that because smart buildings and sustainability are increasingly becoming the norm, other factors like social interaction, placemaking, mixing business and leisure, are becoming more important. Positioning work as a part of everyday life, bringing the workplace to the center of the city, creating people-centric workplaces—all these factors will contribute to increasing engagement.

Bakker concludes by telling us about an article he'd read in the New York Times a little while ago, "where a neuroscientist said that if you give people the opportunity to open a window or to move the furniture around or to change their environment, their cognitive processes are improved by 25 percent, which is huge! So just to be able to give people the opportunity to change the environment, is already an improvement of their workplace. [...] And if people start to be able to be part of the creation of the workspace, then it's a whole new thing. So I think co-creation is the word for the future." **WS**

CASE 3

Microsoft Netherlands

The "Micro Polis" —
encouraging small-scale community building

Twelve years ago, Microsoft Netherlands and its 700 employees moved into a new 10,000㎡ office space. At the time, 9,000㎡ was designated for Microsoft, and 2,500㎡ was semipublic for employee and guest use. Today, however, the numbers are flipped: 6,000㎡ is semipublic, and only 2,000㎡ is reserved for private space. The remaining 3,500㎡ is occupied by the coworking company Spaces.

"We didn't need a large office anymore," René van der Vlugt, Microsoft Netherlands Business and Digital Transformation Lead Director, says. Employees are increasingly working from home or on the go, and many jobs focus on collaboration with clients. "Our product portfolio requires us to work closer with the customer, understand their business, to really help them. That's why we have more customer space."

Of course, this means there is no longer technically enough designated space per employee, but conveniently. Spaces can serve as an overflow area when employee numbers are higher, depending on factors like ABW, season, or time of day. Its other key function is to attract AI startups, one of Microsoft's focus areas.

The concept behind the office design is the idea of the "micro polis." As Francesco Messori, creative director of D/DOCK, the company that designed the building interiors, explains: "We need an office, because an office is a community.

Microsoft Netherlands
Amsterdam [The Netherlands]
Founded: 1975
Employees: 131,000 (2018)
Revenue: 110.36 billion (2018)
*Data applies to company worldwide

The layout of the 6,000㎡ semipublic floor, also known as "the Motherboard." The space is accessible to employees, clients, and partners. Fully equipped with meeting rooms, a cafeteria, and a room in the center for 360-degree projection mapping, called the Holosuite.

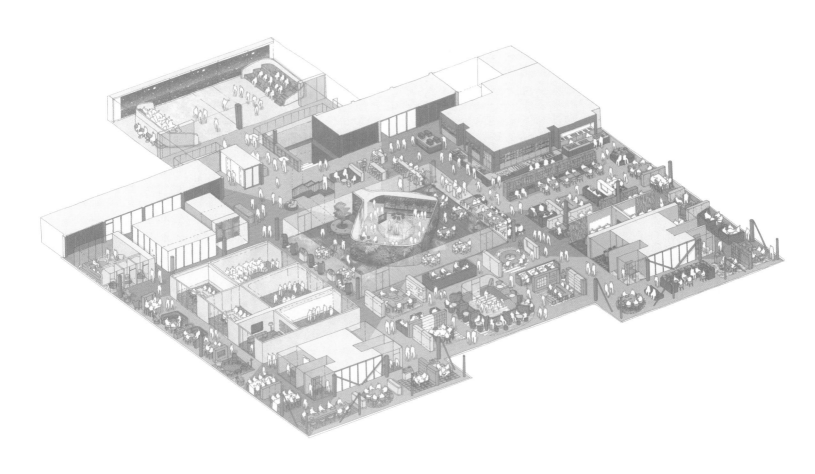

An office is a place where you meet somebody else, you share things, you experience serendipities or unexpected encounters." The idea was to distribute different types of spaces within the building, so people with a diverse range of values can congregate in different "poleis" in their own preferred work spaces, and connect with each other organically, creating micro communities in the process. This is why no two rooms are alike.

We asked Van der Vlugt to explain the reason behind the radical change to the office space. As he explains, the first is to best manage work-life balance. Things like bringing in work that can be done at home, or checking work messages during time off, for example. "We started this initiative where we say, you need to work smarter, not harder. It's kind of the simple line we took." The other reason is to address the changing nature of client collaborations. Each team adjusts their work method depending on the type of collaboration they have with each client. It was the natural course of things for employees to seek a more flexible and expansive space to work in.

As a tech company, naturally Microsoft is advancing its digital technology to build smarter offices. More than 1,000 sensors throughout the building monitor things like temperature, lighting, humidity, carbon dioxide concentration, and room usage, as well as the whereabouts of employees. "We're now in the phase where we see it as an IoT solution," Van der Vlugt notes. How to make the sensors

©Michael van Oosten

1. A private space reserved for Microsoft employees. Employees can also use the semipublic spaces, but often opt to work here when they need to focus. Complete with a raised tatami-mat seating area, it is a designated quiet space.

2. An area available for both guests and employees; security is one step higher than in the semipublic spaces. The space is adorned with artwork that stimulates the senses.

3. The exterior of the office building that Microsoft moved into 12 years ago. Feeling the need for a more client-oriented space, renovations were initiated when the lease was renewed in summer 2017. The office is located in an area of exhibition centers and office buildings near the Schipol airport.

4. A spacious cafe in the semipublic area. Shared amenity spaces create opportunities for collaboration among Microsoft employees, guests, and the coworking entity Spaces tenants.

smarter? How to best control the building's heating system? Is it possible to start warming the building earlier on colder days? There are countless ways to utilize the data, but improving office operations is certainly an important goal. Conference room booking is a good example; at Microsoft, 42 percent of recurring meetings don't actually take place in their reserved rooms. "We're trying to see how to change people's behaviors to be more efficient with our square meters," Van der Vlugt says.

Hospitality is another important theme. "Hospitality is of course the link, the key element of this office, which also in my opinion is the future of [the] work environment," Messori notes. One example is the luxurious hotel suite-type space. Minus a bed and bathroom, it's equipped with everything else necessary to accommodate clients or teams looking to focus for a couple of days, or take a more comfortable break. A mere hour working in a conference room equipped only with the usual chairs and tables can be draining, but this type of space enables a more appealing space to work in. This type of space is referred to as a "bleisure" suite, a cross between business and leisure, and is sprinkled throughout the building. In other words, the office of the future is no longer just a box for working inside of, but is reemerging as an intelligent "personal assistant" that supports employees in their different work styles as they go about their day. **WS**

René van der Vlugt
Business and Digital
Transformation Lead Director
Microsoft Netherlands

Francesco Messori
Creative Director and
Partner
D/DOCK

An office space open to clients and partners

2007

Semi-public spaces — 2,500㎡ (21.7%)

Private spaces — 9,000㎡ (78.3%)

2018

Coworking spaces — 3,500㎡ (30.4%)

Private spaces — 2,000㎡ (17.4%)

Semi-public spaces — 6,000㎡ (52.2%)

5. A section of the semipublic workspace with relaxed sofa seating. Employees can spend the day comfortably while maximizing work performance.

6. A section of the semipublic workspace. Curtains and partitions make it easy to create more privacy as needed. "You can always find a place that fits your mood," Van der Vlugt says.

7. The entrance. Security is understated to maintain a welcoming atmosphere. To the left is a small kitchen where guests can drink coffee as they wait. IDs provide easy access to lockers and dining areas.

8. A restaurant shared with the coworking office Spaces offers guests and employees healthy dining options.

9. A section of the semipublic space, where employees and clients can collaborate as they wish. Each floor features a different design, complete with private rooms and kitchens to accommodate longer stays.

1. Startups occupy some of the private rooms. Each Spaces location has unique features, but this particular location aims to attract AI startups, a clientele that also appeals to Microsoft for collaborations.

2. A corner within the Spaces offices (images 1-6). Outside guests and Microsoft employees intermingle.

3. Meeting booths for smaller groups. Personal desks in the foreground. A variety of workspaces are available to accommodate different preferences.

4. A cafe space in an open area where employees engage in casual conversation.

5. Sofa seating lines a bright window area, overlooking the city planned near the Schipol Airport as a magnet for global companies.

6. An attractive entrance in muted tones welcomes tenants and guests.

FOCUS 2

Data analytics meets workplace design

Zaha Hadid Architects

Uli Blum
Consultant
Zaha Hadid Architects

Joined Zaha Hadid Architects in 2011 after working at Dutch architecture firm OMA Asia and as project director of the Hong Kong office of Gehry Technologies. Currently he is Co-head of ZH Analytics + Insights (ZHAI) with Arjun Kaicker, who was previously a partner at Foster + Partners.

How will data change office design? To explore this question, Zaha Hadid Architects' Uli Blum and his colleague Arjun Kaicker started the Analytics + Insights department in 2015. They combine their expertise as architects and workplace specialists with coding and computational skills. "We think that a design that is not informed by data is just decoration. Worse still designing without data is like driving blindfolded," Blum explains. "It's directionless and even dangerous to make design decisions without analyzing their possible effect on the wellness and performance of the design's users."

Their approach is to learn from online services that mine user data to anticipate user needs and preferences, not unlike the way a company like Netflix learns what users like over time to improve recommendations. This can be applied to the workplace by using machine learning to continually analyze and cross reference variations in spatial and environmental performance across floorplans, patterns of space usage over time, and user feedback on workplace satisfaction and preferences. The goal is to use the data analytics to develop design solutions that both accurately anticipate and effectively support user needs, not just on day one of occupancy but throughout the lifecycle of the building. "If we had such workplaces, I strongly believe it would create much happier, healthier and more successful employees and businesses." Blum says.

For example, many offices today are now using sensors to collect data about building performance. However the most valuable insights this sensor data can provide are often never uncovered, insights that impact not only building performance but employee performance.

Improving building performance is important, but ultimately improving employee performance has a much greater payback. "Given that roughly one percent of the lifecycle cost is the cost to build the building, 9 percent is the cost of maintenance and energy, and 90 percent is in salaries, over the lifetime of a building the greatest financial impact of a workplace is not its upfront cost, or even lifecycle cost, but how it helps or hinders the success of its occupiers," Blum explains. "Making employees 10 percent happier and maybe 10 percent more effective is like being able to build 10 more buildings."

Data can also have a positive impact on interpersonal collaboration and development. Blum and his colleagues' research extracted several revealing facts about office layouts. For example, there is the effect of desk proximity. "There is a well known professor from MIT, Thomas J. Allen, whose research found that communication frequency rapidly decreases with distance. He found that the frequency we interact with co-workers reduces rapidly after 8 meters and is almost negligible after 24 meters." By developing an algorithm that analyzes the walking distance among desks, ZHAI started to see how very small variations in desk design or configuration impact office interaction. Another finding was that corner areas of office towers have the lowest interaction potential, and yet as Blum laments, "Unfortunately companies usually put bosses in the

1. The entrance of Zaha Hadid Architects headquarters. The reception and cafeteria are combined for use as a break area, or for meetings.
2. The board room in the headquarters office. Used for important client meetings.
3. The headquarters work space. The desk of the late founder Zaha Hadid, who died in 2016, is preserved as it was.
4. The building exterior. The office has occupied the same building since its founding in a renovated elementary school in Clerkenwell, an area where many of London's design firms are concentrated. The London office employs about 400 people.

Simulations of office layouts based on various parameters

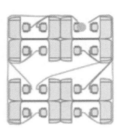

1

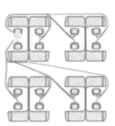

2

43% of desks <8mts away

73% of desks <8mts away

3

Average Humidity

100%
75%
50%
25%
0%

Mon, Jan 22

Average Temperature (°C)

32
24
16
8
0

Mon, Jan 22

Average CO2 (ppm)

1200
900
600
300
0

Mon, Jan 22

Desk Occupancy

100% Peak
75%
50% Average
25%
0%

Fri, Jan 19   Sat, Jan 20   Sun, Jan 21   Mon, Jan 22   Tue, Jan 23   Wed, Jan 24   Thu, Jan 25

Data collected on space usage to perform complex data analysis.

1 A figure showing how visibility and distance changes for different desk shapes.
2 Study of how distances change between employee desks based on different seating layouts.
3 Sensors can monitor variables like temperature, air quality, and desk occupancy, providing realtime measurements for how desks are actually being used.

4

ZH Analytics and Insights

Arts University of Bournemouth | Lower Exhibition Space
24 Hour Movement Sensor Reading

00:00:00

5

6

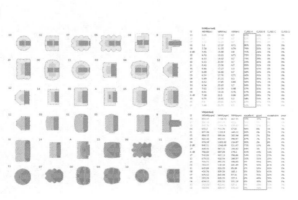

7

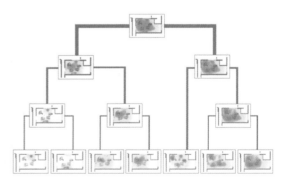
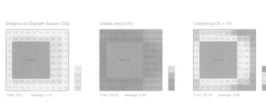

4 Sensors placed in a gallery space capture activity. A "heat map" indicated by red zones indicates areas of high usage.
5 Heat map analysis enables a scientific grouping of how space is being used.
6 Tens of thousands of different scenarios are generated by an algorithm that tests a variety of floor plans.
7 Analysis of optimal placement of the architectural core, based on distance to sources of daylight and visibility.

Visibility per Workspace
Area / Coworker count

Planned, Confident
meetings

Most Visibility
Informal, Unplanned
meetings

Most Privacy

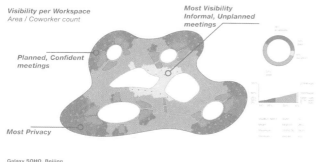

Galaxy SOHO, Beijing
Zaha Hadid Architects

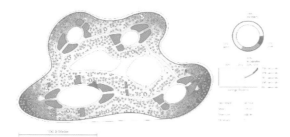

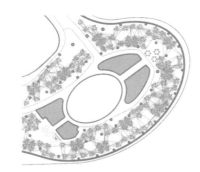

Daylight Penetration
Class A / B / C / D Workspace

Most Time At Desk

Least Time At Desk

Touch down

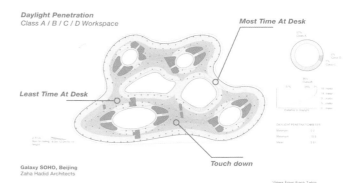

Galaxy SOHO, Beijing
Zaha Hadid Architects

Views From Each Table
120 Degree Cone of View

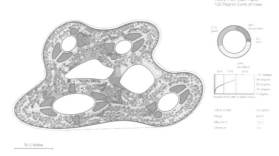

Data analytics applied to Galaxy SOHO in Beijing, a multi-tenant building designed by ZHA. Hundreds of thousands of simulations were generated to examine the impact of parameters such as employee visibility, travel distance, view cone, etc. Though at first glance the shape and placement of the building core may seem arbitrary, it is a logic-based solution derived from careful data analysis.

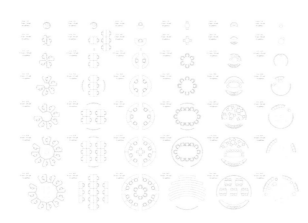

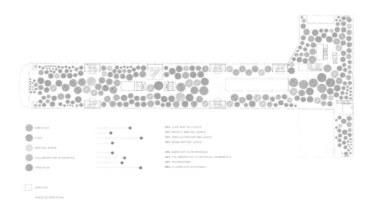

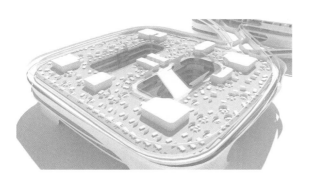

Infinitus Plaza in Guangzhou is another office building designed by ZHA, here shown utilizing the automated office layout algorithm developed by ZHAI. The layout shifts based on user number and scenario type (concentration vs. conversation). Frequency of space use can be monitored through sensors, after which parameters can be adjusted and the layout automatically updated. Through the repetition of this process, the space will be able to learn to self-adjust.

corners." In other words, the people that should be communicating the most, are often placed in the area that has the least potential for communication.

Another important factor to consider for optimizing office space is the quality of the relationship between desks. Naturally, it's easier to communicate with someone who is facing you and often people feel uncomfortable having others looking at them who they can't see. This visual network can have a significant impact on our psychological comfort and yet it is rarely analyzed. Blum explains, "I lived 12 years in Hong Kong and China and I was astonished by all the round tables in restaurants and what a positive impact this had on communication because everyone at the table had an equal view of everyone else." Based on these real-life observations, ZHAI created an algorithm to assess the visual effectiveness of various office layouts. This tool analyzes various aspects of each person's visibility in relation to desk placement. Each desk is given a visual comfort score, which is then used to help reconfigure or allocate the office layout appropriately.

This is not to say that increased data analytics will yield the perfect design solution. "In the past there was this thinking that you created a standard and you rolled it out across your entire office, in a one size fits all approach," Blum says. The thinking was, "If I optimize the work desk and give it to everyone, everyone should be happy; but that's no longer the case." In fact, nowadays having workplace variety is considered vital for productivity because people's preferences for things like lighting and temperature are different. "So really, we need to provide a diverse high quality environment, that allows people to choose the work setting

that is best for them. AI and machine learning allow us to create more diverse work settings and help us understand which setting might best suit us as individuals at any given moment," he concludes.

So how can data best inform office design? Blum suggests that designers make better decisions based on data rather than purely on intuition. Buildings can now be designed to embody solutions based on a huge amount of inputs and parameters, rather than being designed around simplified assumptions and outdated standards. "Using technology gives us the possibility to know more about our design and make better decisions," he says.

While researching and developing data-enhanced office design, a vision has emerged for the office of the future, where Blum believes an office could optimize itself autonomously with the help of sensors, automated design algorithms, and self re-configuring furniture. It could be a network of self-learning workspaces that could mold themselves to the needs of each individual user. Desks, amenity areas and conference rooms could reconfigure overnight, ever-evolving, almost like a organism. And this adaptability need not be limited to functionality of space but also create an ever evolving look and feel. Blum describes his vision for what a future office might look like: "We already have lights that change color over the day so we get the feeling of sunlight. But we may also see the entire office change over time, with the rhythm of the seasons. Maybe the color of furniture changes over time. In spring, when the cherries blossom, you can have a whiter office, in autumn it has kind of earthy tones, and in winter you have cheerful colors so people don't get depressed, and so on." **WS**

1. Blum and the Analytics + Insights team occupy an office space about a 10 minute walk from headquarters. Mathematicians, data scientists, and architects round out the team. Also on the same floor is a team that manages international competition proposals.
2. A gallery on the ground floor showcasing mainly furniture and sculptures designed by Zaha Hadid. Both the gallery and exhibition space in the underground floor are open to the public.
3. The exterior of the 3-story office building that houses the Analytics + Insights department. A panel of windows showcases the gallery space on the first floor.

CASE 4

CIRCL

A major financial institution takes a lead in the circular economy

CIRCL
Amsterdam [The Netherlands]
Completion: 2017
Total area: 3,500㎡
Number of tenant businesses:
Approximately 2,000 (2018)

As the traditional driver of linear capitalist economic growth, banks are undergoing a period of soul searching as the world moves toward more sustainable models. To this end, in 2017 major Dutch bank ABN AMRO created CIRCL, a pavilion dedicated to exploring models of sustainability, directly in front of their headquarters. Merijn van den Bergh, the director of CIRCL, says about this initiative that: "It's not about financial impact only, it's about having a positive impact on society and on the environment." This establishes ABN AMRO Bank as a leader in building a sustainable, circular economy in Europe.

The genesis of the building was rather serendipitous. Plans to build an extension to the ABN AMRO headquarters to address the lack of meeting rooms were already in motion, when the project team proposed a bold move to the Managing Board. The result was CIRCL, a building that aims to achieve the highest sustainability levels in the world. Locals congregate in the building's facilities that are open to the public, including the 10 conference rooms used by ABN AMRO employees and third parties, along with workshops, a restaurant, and a gallery.

1. A panoramic view of the floor. At right is a shop selling sustainable goods, and in back is a restaurant that aims for zero waste. Part of the work lounge is visible at left. Everything in the space is constructed with recycled material.
2. The exterior of the building, located in Zuidas, a business district in Amsterdam. The headquarters of CIRCL's creator ABN AMRO Bank, a major Dutch bank for retail, corporate, and private banking clients based in Amsterdam, is visible in the background.
3. A gallery on the ground floor. There's also a work lounge, shop, and restaurant.
4. The basement level is lined with rooms for meetings and workshops that can be used by citizens and external groups, in addition to ABN employees. It is also used as the main venue for "We Make the City," a large-scale event that investigates the sustainable future of the city.
5. A meeting space in the basement level. Circl Academy, the company's program for teaching employees about the values of the circular economy, was holding a workshop there at the time of our visit.
6. A cafe stand on the basement level used for many occasions, from a break area during events to casual client meetings.
7. An event space in the basement level. The bank's old safes and mailboxes were repurposed and given a new wood finish.

To minimize the environmental impact, mostly recycled materials from other buildings were used for the construction. The soundproofing and insulation in the ceiling was made from 16,000 used jeans and plastic bottles cut into small pieces to support the constructions of the walls, and the furniture was sourced by a company that sells vintage goods.

What's more, each piece of the building's architectural material has a unique ID linking to information on how it might be reused should the building be disassembled. "They didn't use any toxic glues or material for the construction," says Marijn Muller, founder of the firm Cartoni Design that advises CIRCL on interior challenges; "[when] someone decides to rebuild the building, they can take all the parts and reuse them again."

The restaurant at CIRCL is also noteworthy for sourcing all of its ingredients from local farmers. This means chefs must be inventive when creating their daily menus, and adapt to what might be in season that day. They make their own honey, and compost their food waste. "We have a lot of flowers in here, and different flowers, so we have high quality honey. It's also used in the kitchen. We also have

a worm hotel; we put our vegetable garbage into that hotel, and the worms make it compost, and we use the compost for the garden," van den Bergh explains.

Additionally, the restaurant is committed to a zero waste policy, and the chefs get creative to use up all the ingredients and eliminate waste. As van den Bergh explains, "The veggies are the most important thing, but we also have meat and fish, depending on what's offered to our chef. [...] they have some deer in the middle of Netherlands, Oostvaardersplassen[...] we use that meat here." To store food, ingredients are preserved in oil or vinegar and kept at room temperature to limit the need for refrigerators.

CIRCL is a place where ABN AMRO employees, clients, and locals alike can stop by, but it is also a place for educating employees about the circular economy. Circl Academy was created for just that purpose. The program is thriving, with 3,000 employees taking part each year. There are also plans to open the Academy to the public in the future. Participants consider what can be done to improve society by taking actionable steps in their own lives to make their homes and businesses more sustainable.

1. The CIRCL restaurant, which practices zero waste by sourcing local ingredients with fewer food miles, and being diligent about using up ingredients. Health is also a priority and a variety of vegan menu items are available.
2. Refrigerators have been limited from the restaurant to lessen the carbon footprint. Ingredients are preserved in oil and vinegar at room temperature in storage jars.
3. A bar on the second floor. Local rum, gin, and homemade beer and tea are house specialties, and served at regular events held in the space.
4. The bar connects to an outdoor garden, where bees are welcome. Food scraps from the restaurant are used as compost. The plants are native to the Netherlands, and change from season to season.
5. The back of the building. A tiered theater space adjacent to the street is a popular hangout spot for locals.

The value chain of CIRCL's architecture

ALL VALUE CHAIN PLAYERS

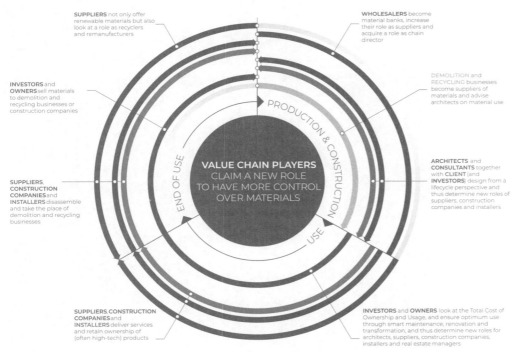

SUPPLIERS not only offer renewable materials but also look at a role as recyclers and remanufacturers

WHOLESALERS become material banks, increase their role as suppliers and acquire a role as chain director

INVESTORS and OWNERS sell materials to demolition and recycling businesses or construction companies

DEMOLITION and RECYCLING businesses become suppliers of materials and advise architects on material use

SUPPLIERS, CONSTRUCTION COMPANIES and INSTALLERS disassemble and take the place of demolition and recycling businesses

ARCHITECTS and CONSULTANTS together with CLIENT (and INVESTORS) design from a lifecycle perspective and thus determine new roles of suppliers, construction companies and installers

PRODUCTION & CONSTRUCTION

END OF USE

USE

VALUE CHAIN PLAYERS CLAIM A NEW ROLE TO HAVE MORE CONTROL OVER MATERIALS

SUPPLIERS, CONSTRUCTION COMPANIES and INSTALLERS deliver services and retain ownership of (often high-tech) products

INVESTORS and OWNERS look at the Total Cost of Ownership and Usage, and ensure optimum use through smart maintenance, renovation and transformation, and thus determine new roles for architects, suppliers, construction companies, installers and real estate managers

The value chain created for CIRCL's construction. Giving each player a larger role than in a conventional method allows for a more sustainable, circular model.

© Circle Economy, Architekten Cie and Circl

How have employees taken to this endeavor to promote a circular economy? "They know they have to, and not everyone knows how; therefore we have an academy, therefore we have a lot of colleagues working on sharing the knowledge, [to] make it more understandable for everyone," van den Bergh replies.

For van den Bergh himself, sustainability was something he used to know nothing about. He now believes it's critical to educate employees about it, even if the process is slow. Starting with small steps for the employees at home and in their private lives, as well as with their customers. "We ask [our customers] to get more sustainable, and we want to help them with our knowledge on sustainability to get more sustainable processes within their companies or private situations."

By building CIRCL, ABN AMRO Bank has made a big statement to the world about their commitment to leading the way to a circular economy, and that statement has been well received. Through the new values this new initiative puts into circulation, employees will continue to bring those changes to the business model itself. Being a catalyst for that shift: this is the true value of CIRCL's mission. **WS**

Merijn van den Bergh
Director
CIRCL

Marijn Muller
Founder
Cartoni Design

Significant reduction of carbon emissions

RENEWABLE ENERGY
28.1t

Renewable energy is generated and supplied at CIRCL, resulting in a carbon emission reduction of 28.1 tons annually. 28.1 tons is equivalent to the amount of emissions from 200 flights between Amsterdam and Paris.

WOODEN CONSTRUCTION
594t

The main structure of CIRCL is made of wood rather than reinforced concrete, which reduces 594 tons of carbon emissions per year. This is equivalent to emissions from 912 roundtrip car rides between Amsterdam and Madrid.

MATERIAL REUSE
813t

Instead of manufacturing and shipping new materials, the building was constructed using only recycled materials, which reduces carbon emissions by 813 tons annually. This is equivalent to the emissions from 3,939 train rides from Amsterdam to Rome.

Environmental technologies CIRCL has invested in

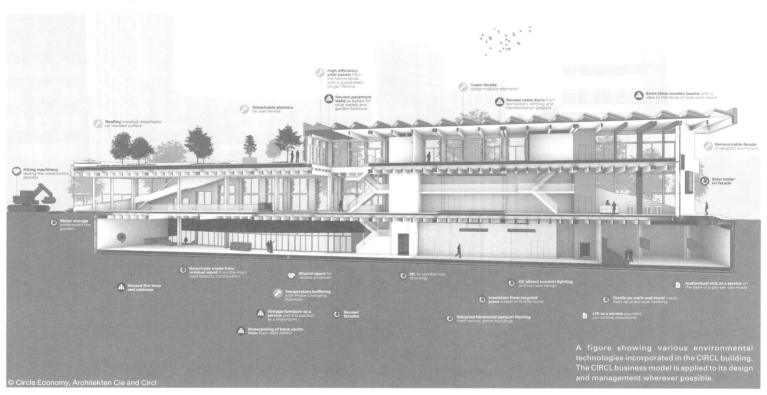

A figure showing various environmental technologies incorporated in the CIRCL building. The CIRCL business model is applied to its design and management wherever possible.

© Circle Economy, Architekten Cie and Circl

CASE 5

B. Amsterdam

One of Europe's largest coworking companies builds a smart city

B. Amsterdam
Amsterdam [The Netherlands]
Completion: 2015
Total area: Approximately 40,000㎡
Tenant businesses: Approximately 300 (2018)

One of Europe's largest coworking companies, B. Amsterdam: three buildings totalling an area of 40,000㎡, with a 100% occupancy rate. Over 300 startups, large corporations, and freelancers congregate in this gigantic platform, which has a large waiting list for an additional 15,000㎡ of space. Most coworking businesses occupy a portion of a tenant building, but one company manages all three buildings at B. Amsterdam—a rarity even in global terms.

This particular building once housed the offices of IBM, but had been empty for over 10 years after IBM moved out. B. Amsterdam opened for business after the building was renovated in 2015. "We started in a completely empty building, only concrete, no water, no electricity, nothing," recalls Ricardo van Loenen, co-founder of B. Amsterdam. There were also no funds, so a university that was shuttering donated a large number of chairs, shelves, and other furniture.

Van Loenen, who is more critical of the type of smart buildings that incorporate technologies such as sensors, says that B. Amsterdam is "really a platform for growth where we bring people together and connect them." The way he sees it, the sensors themselves don't

1. A cafeteria and coworking space. In addition to this open space, freelancers and businesses also occupy private rooms within the complex. The cafeteria is an instrumental hub for community building.
2. The building, which formerly housed the offices of IBM, was fully renovated into what is now called B.1. Located near Schiphol airport, it's surrounded by other office buildings and storage facilities.
3. An area lined with individual desks, used mostly by freelancers.
4. A meeting area in a corner of one of the coworking spaces. Sofa seating creates a relaxed atmosphere.
5. A cafeteria on the ground floor. A large event space in the back provides space for community building inclusive of non-tenants.

change the way people work, nor do they connect people by being in the building. He suspects that having people benefit from meeting each other in person is more important than techie things like automating room temperature.

The tenants at B. Amsterdam tend to feel similarly. This is a coworking space with private offices for startups large and small, and in that sense, it may not be so different from other coworking businesses like WeWork. The true essence of B. Amsterdam, though, is not about an abundance of luxury facilities or a wealth of "smart" technology. The most important thing is that it's a place where people can link up and grow communities organically. Only those who fit the building's philosophy of "growing together" are brought into the building, and the communities they build in turn attract like-minded new members. The meetups, various conferences, and workshops that take place in the office all facilitate opportunities for interaction. "I think WeWork is really a real estate player," van Loenen says, emphasizing that B. Amsterdam has a different approach. "I have no love for real estate, but I have love for the growth of people—so that's a different mindset."

Many large corporations are rushing in to join and become part of the B. Amsterdam community. Currently there are 17 in-house, including Heineken, PwC, and FIFA. Interestingly, even IBM, which used to occupy the same building, is also now a tenant. These companies are all looking to collaborate with startups, who form the nucleus of the ecosystem within the building. As van Loenen explains, "Startups

6. The IBM Innovation Space is leased to IBM, which formerly occupied the building. IBM is also looking to connect with startups to implement new ideas.
7. The IBM work space. The room has a simple structure similar to a greenhouse.
8. A large area leased by the travel agency Hotelchamp. The tenants include companies with over 100 employees like Hotelchamp, as well as freelancers and startups.
9. The offices of Startupbootcamp, an accelerator program that supports rising startups.
10. A bar counter in the restaurant on the fifth floor. The cafeteria on the ground floor is self-service, but full-service is available here.
11. A rooftop park adjacent to the restaurant. Herbs and vegetables are grown in the park, which has a total area of 1,600㎡.
12. The interior of Smart City Hub. An expansive space used to construct an ecosystem for the entire building.
13. Smart City Hub is located in a renovated storage building adjacent to B.1. The aim is to create a circular economy within the campus by attracting startups that are smart-city oriented.

need to have clients, but also need the power of the corporations, and together they can thrive."

After B. Amsterdam was founded in 2014, the speed at which it grew was surprising, even to van Loenen himself. The rapid growth meant the community of B. Amsterdam was limited by the confines of the building itself. Currently, the company is planning to meet the demand by expanding into a larger area and creating a smart city zone.

Step one of this initiative is to create a 1,800㎡ farm on the property. Eventually, the ingredients from the farm will be served at the in-house restaurant. Waste will be reused. Houses will be built to support lifestyles that use only a small amount of water and electricity. The B. Smart City Hub, set in a renovated storage space, will attract smart city-oriented startups. The goal here is to test out every potential solution for building a sustainable city.

"The dream first was to create a city within the building," van Loenen says, but that dream rapidly became a reality. "Now we want to create the city of the future within this area. [We're] working hard for it." **WS**

Ricardo van Loenen
Co-Founder
B. Amsterdam

1. One of the company's three buildings, B.3. Formerly used by Nissan, this building was also completely renovated to house tenant businesses. Pictured is a cafeteria on the top floor serving healthy meals.
2. The exterior of B.3. The protruding section of the building is the boardroom pictured in image 3.
3. The B. 3 boardroom is a shared meeting space for the building, leased out to tenants as needed.
4. Contemporary art adorns the B.3 common areas. The atmosphere here is slightly more refined compared to the more casual B.1.
5. A floor lined with the private offices of B.3 tenants. The greenery and wood floors give the space a natural look.

FOCUS 3

A new unit for building "smart" that will transform the city of the future

The Smart Precinct

Jeremy Myerson
Director
Worktech Academy

World-renowned expert in the study of workplace design. Director of Worktech Academy and Helen Hamlyn Center for Design at the Royal College of Art. Member of design organization advisory boards in South Korea, Switzerland, and Hong Kong.

The smart precinct is a concept researched by Jeremy Myerson, a world-renowned expert in the study of workplaces. Here the unit of "smart" refers not to a building or a city, but to a precinct, defined as an area encompassing 2-3 blocks, that can be managed by a single developer. As Myerson sees it, "The most important thing about the smart precinct is that it's a very manageable unit to organize and plan for."

Because a smart precinct is in-between the macro scale of a city, and the micro scale of a single building, it can maximize its impact. Smart cities are unwieldy to manage because their complexity crisscrosses the jurisdiction of city municipalities and government, while smart buildings can be too small to make a significant impact beyond its own walls. A smart precinct, then, is just right: small enough to manage, large enough to have an impact beyond the footprint of the building itself.

An important concept to apply to the smart precinct is the "intermix," a strategy that aims to connect different communities—residential with offices, public with private, virtual with real—to create diverse, mixed-use areas. Within such a smart precinct, data is collected to provide users with customized services and a range of shared amenities within striking distance. "For the meetings, for food, why have your own canteen? Why not just go into a precinct where there's lots of food places around?" Myerson says.

Smart precincts can be grouped into four general types. The first is the enterprise model, which is driven by large corporations and anchored around workspaces. Other entities such as retail, entertainment, hospitality, and university facilities are added to the mix, to round out the precinct. An example is South Eveleigh (formerly Australian Technology Park), developed by the Australian property group Mirvac,

The Concept of "Intermix"

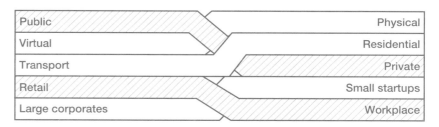

The idea that the fabric of a precinct can be strengthened by combining polarized entities, such as virtual and physical space, large corporations with startups, public with private entities.

The changing role of the developer

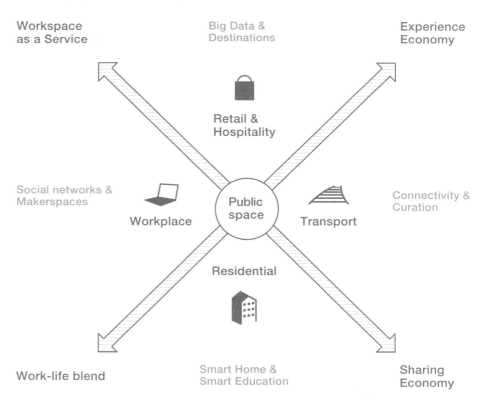

A figure showing how the idea of the intermix responds to new work trends and technologies. For example, smartphone applications and digital check-ins are increasingly used in the workplace, as well as in the retail and hospitality industries.

which partnered with Myerson on the smart precinct research project. The site houses several large corporations, as well as a range of entertainment and hospitality facilities.

The second is the emporium model, where up to 50 percent of the space is dedicated to retail. Myerson gives London's Westfield Stratford City as an example of this type: "Maybe 20 percent is residential, 20 percent workspace, 20 percent culture, education and leisure," he says. The shopping center is located in the midst of university and office buildings, and is near the London Court of International Arbitration (LCIA). Consumers are drawn to the center's many entertainment facilities; data is collected in real time from the businesses, and

utilized to make improvements to the precinct. "It's also about well-being and fitness and access to gyms, and having a social life [...] The irony is that Japan has actually done a lot of very good mixed-use developments, but it hasn't put the workspace at the center of it [...] It's kept the working place separate."

The third is the haven model, which is residentially driven. "Dormitory towns in the day are dead in the same way that central business districts at night are dead, so what they're trying to do is create a residential in the middle of very vibrant smart precinct [...] this is where the digital overlay of the smart precinct is helping people as they age well in place, but it also allows people to work from home," Myerson explains.

The interchange model is the fourth type, which is built around transportation hubs. A good example is London's King's Cross Station; buildings are positioned around the station, and real-time data is streamed to the offices within the precinct.

What is the ideal size for a smart precinct? Myerson gives the example of King's Cross, with 1,800 residential units, as a good example of scale versus density to generate effective data. "Too small and you're talking about a cluster of small buildings; it's not really a smart precinct, and you can't get the diversity of use. [...] King's Cross is 67 acres. I think that's probably the maximum," he explains.

Currently, smart precincts are redefining the role of the office

building of the future. "The office building is one of the building blocks of the smart precinct. It's still there, but it's not hermetically sealed from the outside. It's porous to the outside, it's permeable to the outside," Myerson explains. He thinks the implementation of more smart precincts will mean that office buildings will be used more as a meeting place, and less as a place equipped with individual desks, because those kinds of spaces will be available within the precinct rather than contained within one building. "People will be coming to these office buildings to meet other people and interact, because they can work anywhere. So I think they're going to change, they're going to look more like hotel lobbies and less like traditional offices." **WS**

Typical models of smart precincts

1. The Enterprise Model

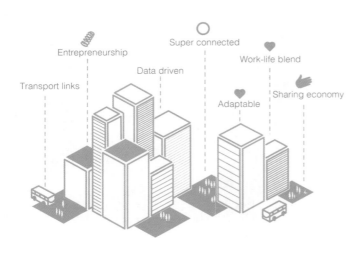

2. The Emporium Model

3. The Haven Model

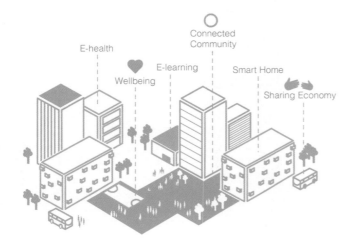

4. The Interchange Model

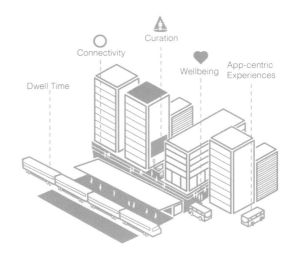

CASE 6

Superblocks

Taking back the streets for Barcelona's citizens

Superblocks
Barcelona [Spain]
Implementation: 2016

Cities were originally built for people. On the streets of Barcelona, it was once common to see people using the streets to do everyday chores, such as preparing their meals. But much like other cities around the world, Barcelona has long since been overtaken by cars.

The superblock is the solution proposed by the city of Barcelona to solve the issue of vehicles taking over spaces that were once inhabited by people. Returning the city to the citizens has made the city healthier, more sustainable, and smarter.

Superblocks are composed of a grid of streets that form a polygon and contain several blocks, and are implemented to adapt to each territory. In the case of Barcelona, the mechanism is very simple, and based on the orthogonal grid of Barcelona (Cerdá Plan)—an innovative idea by the city planner Ildefons Cerdá dating back to the mid-19th century. Here, the interior of a set of nine blocks is closed to regular traffic and gives preference to residents' bicycles and pedestrians. The streetscapes within the parameters were also reshaped based on resident preferences. There are parks, greenery, and ample spaces for residents to enjoy their neighborhood. The aim of all of this, according to Barcelona City Sustainability Officer Neda Kostandinovic, is to give priority to people and sustainable mobility such as bicycle use and public transportation, and decrease the use of cars city-wide by 21 percent.

Looking back at the history of Barcelona over the past half century, the superblock has even more depth in light of the three major changes the city has undergone. First, there was the collapse of the Spanish dictatorship in 1975 and the introduction of democracy. Then in 1992, the city hosted the Barcelona Olympics, spurring development of major highways and other important infrastructure. And then the post-Olympic era of rapid development after 1992. The grid-like city had been designed with public comfort in mind, including factors like sunshine and air quality. Even so, the city had reached its limit. While it's recommended that 10㎡ of green space be allocated per citizen, now there is only 6.64㎡. The heat island phenomenon is also serious, with temperatures rising by a full 4 degrees in the city center and surrounding areas. Noise and exhaust emissions from automobiles also exceed the standards set by the World Health Organization.

But there's the small issue that the there is nowhere left to build green space in city of Barcelona. Thus the idea of the superblock was re-introduced; this could be a way to improve quality of life without drastically changing the shape of the city.

The implementation of the superblock is done in three levels. The first, the basic level, is centered on mobility changes. For example, signs for pedestrian priority areas are placed on each road, and car access

1. Aerial view of Barcelona. The block-shaped grid is clearly visible from above. The superblock combines nine blocks into one unit and redevelopes it to improve civic life.
2. El Poblenou district where the superblock was introduced (also images 3-7). The plan transformed what used to be an intersection into a park. Public spaces are utilized to the fullest, such as al fresco dining throughout the district on weekends.
3. Charging station for EVs (electric vehicles) installed on the street. Barcelona actively promotes the use of EVs to stave off noise and air pollution.
4. A rollerblader skates down a street painted like a running track. Because car access is limited, pedestrian areas have increased dramatically.
5. A former intersection is now a park. Fully equipped as a playground, it now attracts children who were not previously seen playing in the area.
6. Benches installed on the former road, arranged in a circle to encourage conversations.
7. Vehicular access within the superblock is strictly controlled. Traffic volume has decreased, allowing easier access for public services such as garbage trucks and buses.

is restricted by time. The second level is tactical urbanism, which aims for minimal intervention using simple methods such as installing playground equipment, benches, plants, and paint. The third level is the structural level. This is the stage where large-scale construction plans are drawn to rebuild city structures, such as sidewalks and roads.

A major difference here compared to other smart cities around the world is the level of citizen participation. City planning inevitably changes citizens' lifestyles, and people can become overwhelmed by big changes to their environment. This is why, as Ariana Miquel, Superblocks Coordinator for Barcelona City Council, says, "We want to involve citizens from the very beginning of the superblocks implementation program through citizen participation process. Neighbors are the ones who know the best the territory." In the Poblenou district, where the tactical urbanism of the superblocks was first introduced in 2016 without proper citizen participation, residents were initially furious. To correct this error, the city made sure to include citizen participation from the beginning when implementing superblocks in the Sant Antoni district. In this way, Barcelona's citizens are regaining control of their city through active participation. **WS**

1. El Poblenou district. Trees and benches have taken over the intersection. There were concerns that the changes would decrease convenience and drive housing values down, but now with the exception of car dealers the response has been overwhelmingly positive.
2. The Sant Antoni district after the superblock was introduced. The public area is centered around the Sant Antoni market, which was renovated in 2018 for the first time in nine years. This superblock has now reached the third stage of implementation, and the layout of sidewalks and roads has been modified drastically.

Ariadna Miquel
Superblocks Coordinator
Barcelona City Council

Neda Kostandinovic
Urban Ecology
Barcelona City Council

The social impact of the superblock

Test calculations* of the social impact after superblocks are expanded from the current six locations to 503 locations as originally planned. *according to Barcelona Institute for Global Health

 Premature deaths
667 PEOPLE

 Ambient levels of NO_2
24%

 Average life expectancy
200 Days

How to Build a Superblock

Conventional Model

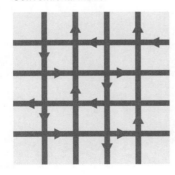

Roads are one-way, which encourages speeding and increased noise and pollution.

Superblocks Model

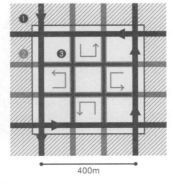

400m

❶ Select 9 adjacent blocks from the Cerdá plan
❷ Turn the four interior blocks from one way to two
❸ Renovate the enclosed former streets into pedestrian-friendly spaces

How to Introduce a Superblock

Level 3: Structural Level	Based on the results of various experiments such as tactical urbanism, the structure of the city is fundamentally rebuilt through long-term construction. The renewal of the Sant Antoni neighborhood is an example of this final stage of completion.

Level 2: Tactical Urbanism	Rather than initiating major construction to reroute roads, existing paved roads are renovated with minimal interventions such as installing playground equipment and benches, and repainting the roads. The El Poblenou district is currently at this level.

Level 1: Basic Level	This level rearranges traffic patterns. At this stage, time restrictions are introduced for vehicular traffic, and signs are placed on each road to prioritize pedestrian usage throughout the superblock.

FOCUS 4

From global to local:
building economic activity from the ground up

Fab City

Tomás Díez
Director
IAAC / Fab Lab Barcelona

From Caracas, Venezuela. Urbanist specializing in
the impact of digital technologies in society, and
Director of the master in Design for Emergent
Futures at IAAC (Institute for Advanced Architecture
of Catalonia)

1. Inside IAAC's main building. The school is a
unique graduate program founded in 2001 to
research a new era of architecture. Student
projects are on display throughout the building.
2. The IAAC Fab space equipped with large
machinery to produce student projects.
3. The IAAC Fab Lab Barcelona work space.
4. IAAC main building exterior. The campus is
located in the former industrial zone of Poblenou
(two locations) and in the Green Fab Lab outside
the city in Valldaura.

Fab City is a global initiative to return the site of manufacturing to local cities. As one of the leaders of this movement, Barcelona-based Fab Lab's director Tomás Díez explains, this reverses the expansion of the late-capitalist production/consumption model from the global scale to the hands of the local community, so that the manufacturing sites of food, energy, and goods can be brought closer to where they are consumed.

Globalization has resulted in the dispersal of sites of production, consumption, and disposal to locations around the world. Considering the fossil fuels required to move materials between these far-reaching sites, the carbon footprint is vast. Díez also says this model is "Making people more dependant on supply chains that are less transparent." Fab City aims to reverse this trend.

The question is, how should this reversal be implemented? Díez notes that "In the case of a smart city, it was a concept that was trying to bring the technology, ICT, or digital technologies to cities, and the main mistake of this approach has been taking this very top-town [approach] in how to implement it." This means that the benefits of smart cities are largely only enjoyed by companies that supply the technology, rather than the citizens that inhabit those very cities. "The government has been embracing the 'smart city' approach as a way to control the city, which I think is stupid," Díez says. Cities are constantly in flux, and in ways that are far more organic than the speed at which smart technology can be implemented top-down.

In contrast, Fab City aims for an implementation that is more flexible and decentralized. In this type of bottom-up approach, the 1,700 fab labs or maker spaces around the world becomes the infrastructure, "connecting with people, and they have a local impact," Díez says. This has the potential to transform citizens from consumers into creators.

In fact, 34 cities around the world have already been designated as Fab Cities, aligning with the idea that what is consumed by the city should be manufactured in the city. This is the result of local Fab Lab communities organizing for government support around the movement, such as in Kamakura City in Japan.

However, full-scale implementation is yet to come. Implementing changes at the scale of the city is complex, and there's a lot of governmental red tape to get through. In Barcelona, for example, Fab City prototypes are being tested on the smaller and more manageable scale of a district. There is the "Made Again Challenge" project with SPACE 10, an open innovation lab at IKEA. The challenge helped to imagine for the first time the Poblenou District as a Fab City Prototype, and was later turned into public policy as the Maker District by the local policy makers. These efforts in Poblenou join the public network of Fab Labs of the city (Fabrication Athenaeums), also created by Fab Lab Barcelona and the Barcelona City Council. IAAC (the independent graduate program Institute for Advanced Architecture of Catalonia that hosts Fab Lab) started the Green Fab Lab just outside the

city to research the theory and practice of a recycling economy of energy, food, and goods.

There are also cities that are adding Fab Labs to the public infrastructure in cities such as Barcelona, São Paulo, and Seoul.

What is next for Fab City? So far, IAAC and Fab Lab Barcelona, directed by Díez, have been leading the way. In recent years, local groups are starting their own movements all over the world. There are Fab City collectives running workshops and conducting research, Fab City networks that bring together the public and private sectors in designated Fab Cities, and institutionalized Fab City foundations that will finance the development of these cities.

Díez has a grand vision for a sustainable future of the Fab City. "What is next is to develop the Fab City Full Stack, which consists of different levels of layers and complementary strategies, programs, actions, and projects, that are needed to achieve such a complex project as the Fab City Global Initiative. The Full Stack is allowing us to unpack the big vision into smaller pieces and builds from existing programs and projects such as the Fab Academy, Public Fab Lab Networks, or Fab City Prototypes. We are also aware that we need to support the configuration of a distributed organization that can operate globally such as the Fab City Foundation, and align efforts with wider networks beyond makers and technologists." **WS**

Green Fab Lab, a project of IAAC and the Fab City Network, with a directive to learn directly from the natural world for 21st century urban renewal. Outfitted with laboratories that produce energy, food, and goods, the lab develops projects and academic programs in collaboration with major research centers around the world

A scene from the "Made Again Challenge" in Barcelona. Participants included SPACE 10 and IKEA designers, and local and overseas makers. The aim of this trial project was to reuse and remake discarded materials within a localized area.

Compacting logistics

PITO to DITO

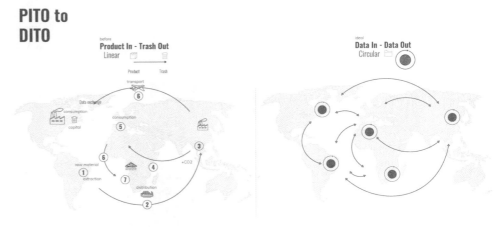

©Tomas Diez in collaboration with Kate Armstrong

Rescaling Global Manufacturing

RESCALING GLOBAL MANUFACTURING

Figure showing the relationship between supply chain and distance. Fab City aims to keep circulation within a 1-10km radius.

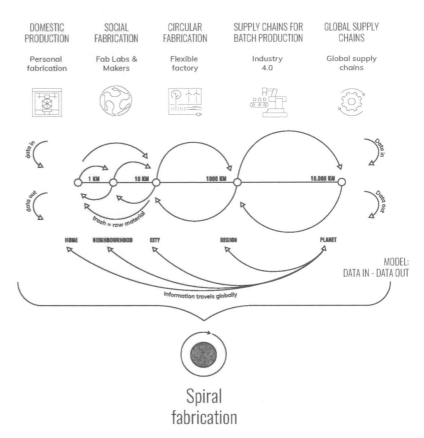

©Tomas Diez in collaboration with Kate Armstrong

FOCUS 5

The data commons:
Taking back control of our data

DECODE

Pablo Aragón
Researcher
DECODE

Data scientist specializing in data analysis of social and political phenomena. Participates in DECODE as a researcher stemming from his interest in grassroots movements and participatory democracy.

A reality of the contemporary age is that data generated by citizens are managed and controlled by global corporations. Ownership of one's personal information, something that should be a fiercely protected asset in the information age, is out of the individual's hands. This is a point of contention in discussions around smart cities. There's the argument that data should be used freely and used to improve services, but in Europe the mainstream opinion is that the sovereignty of personal information should be returned to individuals.

DECODE (DEcentralised Citizen-owned Data Ecosystems) comes out of that philosophy. It's a pilot program in the EU that examines how open and personal data can be used socially beyond the restrictions of the GDPR (General Data Protection Regulation), which has strict regulations regarding the protection of personal information. Currently, large-scale social experiments are underway in two cities: Barcelona and Amsterdam, and run on Barcelona's free, open-source digital democracy software called Decidim. "The aim of DECODE," data scientist and DECODE researcher Pablo Aragón says, "is to provide an infrastructure to allow citizens to control data they produce, and also to exploit in a common way that data."

In general, there are two ways this is done. One is by protecting personal data on the platform. The second is by sharing information on an open-source platform that can be accessed by anybody. DECODE is paving the way to a third option, a community-driven platform between individuals and organizations known as the data commons. The data collected here is used for the common good, and the process is fully transparent to the public.

Here are a few examples of recent experiments in Barcelona. One is a trial of decentralized democracy using personal data. Decidim, a participatory democracy platform developed by Barcelona City, was incorporated into the DECODE infrastructure to allow citizens to sign policy proposals directly through the DECODE app. In addition, personal information such as gender, age range, and district remains confidential. Conventionally, data that can't be captured because of confidentiality rules can be collected on a voluntary basis and used to determine vital demographics. The other is a trial where citizens themselves create the data. Because the public has become more aware that processing noise data can lead to the leaking of personal information, there's a growing movement to create rules and protocols that better protect personal information.

In smart cities, public data is collected via sensors placed throughout the city by local governments and companies, who own and manage the data in a top-down approach.

In contrast, through participation in DECODE, it's the public that is in control of their own data. This is the bottom-up approach, because the public acquires and manages their own data, and collectively obtains value from that data as needed for the common good. In the words of Aragón, this initiative is "a transition from this top-down extractivist idea of the smart city, to the bottom-up democratic city." **WS**

Decidim: Participatory democracy platform

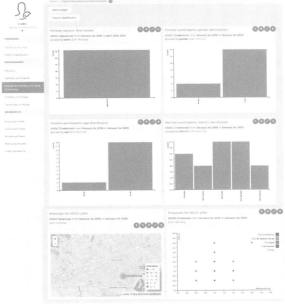

Free open-source participatory democracy for cities and organizations launched by Barcelona City Council. By working with DECODE, voter attribute data can be collected voluntarily and anonymously to provide demographic statistics.

Transforming the relationship between data and citizens to a bottom-up model

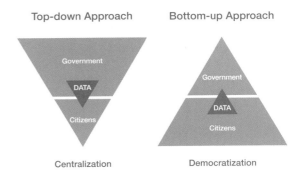

Citizens who meet the conditions volunteer personal information through DECODE. This includes valuable information such as which demographic groups participated in policy-making.

The DECODE pilot project workshop was held in Barcelona.
©Smart Citizen at Fab Lab Barcelona

Spaceship "Self":
Re-examining Ownership in the Digital Age

Editor-in-Chief: Shotaro Yamashita

The smart workplace movement continues to gain momentum.
Where did it originate, and where is it headed next?
What is needed in the era of the data-optimized workplace?

An Ever-Expanding Digital Platform

As the focus on well-being in the workplace over the last several years moves into the mainstream, the next topic on the horizon is the idea of the technology-enabled smart workplace. There are three main factors driving this momentum.

The first is the shift to user experience. Similar to how app-driven Uber transformed the taxi industry, in Western countries rapid digital disruption is bringing massive shifts to the very structure of industry. Demand for tech-savvy young talent is high, especially millennials and generation Z who grew up using highly customizable digital tools. These younger generations will want to be in workplaces that accommodate a high degree of flexibility, driving the current need to consider the preferences of the individual user.

The second factor is sustainability. Formerly considered more of a social responsibility and secondary cost of economic growth, the thinking now is that unmitigated economic growth and environmental protection are simply not compatible. New economic models are increasingly necessary, such as Oxford University's Kate Raworth's visual model of a more sustainable Doughnut Economics, and MIT professor Erik Brynjolfsson's idea of GDP-B—where the B stands for the "benefits" of digital services that are not paid for by the user as a more accurate economic indicator of Gross

Shotaro Yamashita

Director of the Workstyle Lab. at Kokuyo Co., Ltd.
Researcher and consultant on the future of the
workplace. Visiting research fellow at The Helen
Hamlyn Centre for Design at the Royal College of
Arts in England, 2016-2017.

Domestic Product. Meanwhile human activity has become the primary influence on the global climate, resulting in the naming of our current geological era as the anthropocene (anthropo-, meaning "human," and -cene, meaning "new"). Simply put, the proactive use of technology to create sustainable workplaces is no longer a performative display of social responsibility, but a non-negotiable necessity.

The third factor is the technological advances that have made smart buildings easier to implement. Though a data-driven society has long existed as an ideal, technological hurdles and costs of data collection and analysis has inhibited real-world application. This is starting to change. From sensor- and transmission-equipped IoT data collection, to the cloud that enables storage of that data, to AI that analyzes it, all have enabled a smoother flow of data. This data ecosystem enables advanced simulations of real-world situations called a digital twin that can be tested quickly and efficiently in virtual space, then implemented cost effectively in the real world.

These factors are fueling the advancement of smartification, but where is it headed? Though environmentally conscious "smart buildings" have existed since the 1990s, current thinking around building the "smart" workplace is centered around optimizing worker experience. With laptops and smartphones enabling remote working in an environment where activity-based work (ABW) has become the norm, the office space needs to be attractive not only functionally,

but also as a place that provides quality work and life experiences. As generational and cultural diversity in the workplace continues to increase, so will the types of experiences that the different workers value. The companies included in the previous pages all utilize smartphone apps to accommodate the diverse needs of their workers in what the futurist Philip Ross calls the app-centric workplace. As this issue reveals, in addition to apps, these companies have discovered that the physical workplace itself must also distinguish itself so the office doesn't become obsolete as an appealing place to commute to. In fact, the rise of smartification has grown in tandem with the rise in luxury amenities in offices around the world.

This push toward smartification is coming not from user-facing companies as you might expect, but from real estate developers and affiliates on the supplier end. ABW has effectively decreased the square footage needed for offices, and developers are eager to identify best uses for the leftover space to maximize their profits. This means there is a need to collect more data: the more data is collected, the higher the accuracy of personalization, and the better potential for smartification. Developer smartification advocates therefore have an incentive to expand data collection from a single floor of an office floor to the whole building, and out to the entire city. An example is the IDEA district in Quayside, Toronto, a development project by Alphabet Inc. company Sidewalk Lab that seeks to use data collected from the city under the umbrella of

a digital platform. As Nick Srnicek, author of "Platform Capitalism," explains, digital platforms share four essential characteristics. 1) They are intermediary digital infrastructures that enable different user groups. 2) They rely and thrive on network effects. 3) By offering free products and services, a particular platform could accumulate more users. 4) They deploy the strategy of constant user engagement through attractive presentations of themselves and their offerings. This is done with the end purpose of extracting data from its users. Data begets more data, optimizing the flow between people and things. We find ourselves at the cusp of an era when the physical platforms of architecture and cities built by our predecessors are being usurped by the digital platforms built by tech companies.

Ownership in the Digital Age

Where does the pursuit of convenience by way of these digital platforms lead?

It can't be said that there is currently a cohesive vision for the future of smartification beyond consumer-facing recommendation systems, likely because the initiative is led by the suppliers. In "The Utopia of Rules" and "Bullshit Jobs," economist and anarchist David Graeber vividly describes how bureaucracy subdivides jobs, creating infinitely dry work content, and entrapping workers within narrowly defined parameters. Low engagement of the modern worker is a significant social issue, with man-made systems permeating society and forcing people to function

as parts of the machinery, depriving us of spirit. This phenomenon is mirrored in the societies created by digital platforms.

As we consider the future of a data-driven society, we must weigh our options to determine the advantages and disadvantages of convenience vs. security, freedom vs. challenge. While giving away personal data can provide some degree of customized guidance and access to services that algorithms have determined suits us best, it also results in losing the opportunity to experience life at its randomized fullest—serendipities, subtleties, mistakes, and all. Unless we maintain firm ownership over the way we want to live our lives, the odds that the majority of us will be swept along by a sea of data are high. As featured in this issue, Superblocks and DECODE, backed by a European sense of individualism, have promptly said no to giving away their private data to regain their sovereignty, and have made it their mission to own their individual ways of living and working.

Whether one chooses to leverage or resist the smart workplace all depends on one's life and work choices. The great 20th-century visionary Buckminster Fuller took an interdisciplinary approach across the fields of architecture, chemistry, and ecology to define earth as one seamless system, a spaceship upon which mankind is the passenger. In work and life, in an increasingly data-driven and flattened world (and beyond to the universe!), how far can one individual go in this spaceship called the self? Maybe it's time to take back the controls from big data, and learn to steer our ships ourselves. **WS**

BACK ISSUES

バックナンバー

WORKSIGHTのバックナンバーは、書店、amazon.co.jp または
渋谷ヒカリエ8FのCreative Lounge MOVの店頭にてお買い求めいただけます。

WORKSIGHT
創刊準備号

特集
境界を越える発想

The Hub
博多小学校
三つ葉在宅クリニック
2010年11月12日発行
非売品

SOLD OUT

WORKSIGHT 01

特集
外とのつながりで
発想するオフィス

Zappos／Gore
Ziba／日建設計
ライフネット生命
隠岐郡海士町
2011年10月7日発行
定価1,200円（税抜）

SOLD OUT

WORKSIGHT 02

特集
オーガニック・
コミュニケーション

HOK／Innocent Drinks
Arup／Acne Production
DDB Stockholm
Hyper Island
サイバーエージェント
2012年6月28日発行
定価800円（税抜）

SOLD OUT

WORKSIGHT 03

特集
イントラプレナーシップ
に火をつけろ！

Evernote／Autodesk
Skype
Wikimedia Foundation
Obscura Digital
良品計画／d.school
2012年11月11日発行
定価800円（税抜）

WORKSIGHT 04

特集
オープンイノベーション
で限界を超える

Rovio Entertainment
Aalto Design Factory
Sitra
Deutsche Telekom
MindLab
ReD Associates
2013年6月24日発行
定価800円（税抜）

SOLD OUT

WORKSIGHT 05

特集
ソーシャル・
コネクティビティ

QVCジャパン／GSK
Continuum／Tumblr
Acumen
Green Spaces
2013年12月16日発行
定価800円（税抜）

WORKSIGHT 06

特集
レジリエント・
ワークスタイル

NHN Entertainment
Singapore Telecom
Seoul Creative Lab
id KAIST／Asiance
The Co
2014年10月1日発行
定価800円（税抜）

WORKSIGHT 特別号

特集
これからの働く環境を
考える7つの視点

Design／Management
Innovation Technology
Facility Management
Learning Environment
Future Insights
2014年12月26日発行
定価700円（税抜）

WORKSIGHT 07

特集
セルフメイド・
フューチャー

Essent／NDSM
Spaces／Royal Dutch
Shell／Waag Society
／Seats2meet.com
2015年4月22日発行
定価800円（税抜）

WORKSIGHT 08

特集
ウェルビーイング・
アット・ワーク

Medibank／NAB
SAHMRI
Macquarie Group
Envato／tacsi
2015年10月16日発行
定価800円（税抜）

WORKSIGHT 09

特集
クリエイティブ
スクールの未来

The York University
The University of
British Columbia
The University of
Toronto／Microsoft
MEC／Telus
2016年4月19日発行
定価800円（税抜）

WORKSIGHT 10

特集
エコシステムを生む
ワークプレイス

Zappos.com,
Downtown Project
SAP, HanaHaus
Square
Dolby Laboratories
Cisco
2016年10月31日発行
定価800円（税抜）

WORKSIGHT 11

特集
スタートアップ都市
ベルリンの
ネクストステップ

betahaus／Factory
Wooga
Axel Springer Plug &
Play Accelerator
IXDS／Tech Open Air
2017年4月24日発行
定価1,000円（税抜）

WORKSIGHT 12

特集
レガシーと
革新のロンドン

Barclays／Sky
The Collective
Level39
Future Cities Catapult
Here East
2017年12月18日発行
定価1,000円（税抜）

WORKSIGHT 13

特集
コミュニティ・ドリブン
都市 ニューヨーク

Kickstarter／Boston
Consulting Group
Vice／A/D/O
Industry City
Pilotworks
2018年6月22日発行
定価1,000円（税抜）

WORKSIGHT 14

特集
台北 集まり方の流儀

CIT
Gamania Group
松山文創園區
FutureWard
Fieldoffice Architects
Taiwan Startup Stadium
PDIS
2019年1月10日発行
定価1,500円（税抜）

WORKSIGHT 特別号

特集
Studio O+Aが生んだ
ワークプレイス新時代

McDonald's／Slack
Blend
Cambridge Associates
Microsoft／Abaca
Giant Pixel
Alibaba Group
2019年7月25日発行
定価1,800円（税抜）